CLIENTS
FIRST

CLIENTS FIRST

THE TWO WORD MIRACLE

Joseph Callaway
JoAnn Callaway

WILEY

John Wiley & Sons, Inc.

Published by John Wiley & Sons, Inc., Hoboken, New Jersey.
Published simultaneously in Canada.

For general information on our other products and services or for technical support, please contact our Customer Care Department within the United States at (800) 762-2974, outside the United States at (317) 572-3993 or fax (317) 572-4002.

Wiley publishes in a variety of print and electronic formats and by print-on-demand. Some material included with standard print versions of this book may not be included in e-books or in print-on-demand. If this book refers to media such as a CD or DVD that is not included in the version you purchased, you may download this material at http://booksupport.wiley.com. For more information about Wiley products, visit www.wiley.com.

Library of Congress Cataloging-in-Publication Data:

3 2140 00331 2945

Callaway, Joseph, 1943-
    Clients first: the two word miracle/Joseph Callaway, JoAnn Callaway.—1st ed.
        p. cm.
    Includes index.
    ISBN: 978-1-118-41277-0 (cloth)
    ISBN: 978-1-118-43175-7 (ebk)
    ISBN: 978-1-118-43177-1 (ebk)
    ISBN: 978-1-118-43179-5 (ebk)
        1. Customer services—United States.   2. Customer relations—United States.
    3. Success in business—United States.   I. Callaway, JoAnn, 1944-   II. Title.
    HF5415.5.C355 2012
    658.8'12—dc23

                                                                2012015374

Printed in the United States of America

10 9 8 7 6 5 4 3 2 1

This book is dedicated to the Clients of Those Callaways.

You taught us everything.

Contents

Acknowledgments

We wish to thank all the Clients of Those Callaways to whom this book is dedicated. Without you our technology would be powerless, our phones would be mute, and our hearts would be empty. Thank you again and again.

The support from our Those Callaways Team has been wonderful. Your tireless service is a tribute. You have carried the *Clients First* torch and we learn from you every day.

Thank you to our first reader and Associate Broker, Marge Lindsay, who, after reading the manuscript, opened her feedback, "With all my heart I love this book." You brought us joy.

Thank you to our longtime client and the most insightful, sardonic, and outspoken person we know, Paul Sharpe. You said you expected it to be one long ad and then you embarrassed us with praise.

Thank you to our *Arizona Republic* account executive, Connie Sana. You were the first to say *Clients First* may change the world.

Thank you to our Title company executive, Michelle Schwartz. Your enthusiasm is contagious and your belief gave us courage.

From the out-of-left-field department we wish to thank our granddaughter, January Harshe, and her husband Brandon, a "Y generation" couple seeking to establish a medical practice in Childress, Texas. We only shared the manuscript with you because you asked. Brandon's subsequent letter of appreciation and your phone calls told us this was a book for all generations and all pursuits. Thank you.

Our reader group was supposed to remain small and kept confidential but our best, laid plans wilted in the face of buzz and excitement, creating a second reader group to whom we owe a deep debt of gratitude. Your feedback spurred us on. Thank you to Bob

Bass, Steve Chader, Brian Critchfield, Jennice Doty, Casey Doty, Jeffrey Fine, Ken Goodfellow, Billy Jensen, Michael Orr, Diane Scherer, Jim Sexton, Toni McCarty, Michael Tiers, Brenda Visser, Heidi Zebrow, and John Zidich.

Thank you Gary Keller. You inspire so many. A special thank you to Jay Papasan. Your thoughts and perceptions were invaluable.

Finally, we wish to express our appreciation to Richard Narramore, our senior editor at John Wiley & Sons, Inc. You are a shining example of *Clients First*, the greatest compliment we can confer.

Introduction

Clients First is the story of our personal journey in real estate. It is a remarkable journey filled with both spectacular highs, as the real estate market bubbled in 2005, and heartbreaking lows, as the bubble burst, creating the worst real estate recession since the Great Depression. Along the way we made a discovery that changed us and everyone around us. We found a miracle. It was the secret to immense business success, and it made everything easy.

This was more than a miracle that occurs once and confounds the philosophers afterward. This was a practical miracle that could be conjured up at will and replicated, not only by us but also by others. It could be passed on to our team, our vendors, our corporate family, our clients, and now to you.

It doesn't matter whether you are the CEO or the newest hire starting out in the mailroom, this book can change your life. *Clients First* may be applied in any endeavor with surprising success.

In Part I of *Clients First*, a memorable lady in a blue suit asks JoAnn, "What is the *real* reason for your fabulous success?" Her query prompts JoAnn and me to carefully analyze what we do so we can give the question a constructive response. In the process, and after years of struggle, we identify the three keys that unlock the secret to putting our clients first. We shine a spotlight on each key so you can quickly grasp the *who*, *what*, *where*, *why*, and *how* of each one. We show how these three complement one another and how they work together to create unimaginable synergy.

In Part II, we examine the evidence and focus on how these two words—*Clients First*—possess great power. Against the backdrop of a market meltdown we observe how *Clients First* has the power to save our business, transform our business, and grow our business.

Remarkably, *Clients First* is an unchanging calm at the eye of the storm. *Clients First* makes it possible to stay the course and achieve great success. *Clients First* overcomes all obstacles and remains unblemished.

In Part III, you learn how you can put your clients first. You are given a powerful path to follow. If you choose to take it, it will lead to your transformation and empower you to thrive in a *Clients First* world. Moreover, people within your sphere of influence will be transformed, too. There is room for everyone to benefit. Admittedly, this is a mighty promise, but *Clients First* (as a book and as a principle) delivers!

The Search for *Clients First*

Mustang Library

She was the third person in line waiting to speak with JoAnn. She wore a proper blue suit, conservative black pumps, and she had her question ready.

We were casually dressed in pressed jeans and comfortable shoes. This was 1999, our third year in the business, and we were known only to our clients. To the 300 real estate agents in attendance, we were like ghosts. We never put our photos on our business cards. Our ads were just for the homes we listed. All the public ever saw were our yard signs, which displayed the words, THOSE CALLAWAYS. In northeast Phoenix, we had a lot of signs.

Two hours earlier our broker, Marge, gave us an eloquent introduction. She used the crib sheet I had given her.

"JoAnn takes care of the people, and Joseph takes care of the paperwork. Sometimes Joseph takes care of people, but they never let JoAnn take care of paperwork."

The audience laughed, even though it was a little corny. But then, I guess *we* are.

We shared the stage with Russell and Wendy Shaw, who were well known. Russell promotes his real estate business through television and radio commercials and is very entertaining. He kept the crowd laughing, and time flew by.

During the presentation, JoAnn fielded several questions and framed all of her answers around how we take care of our clients.

How do you get listings? Our clients refer us to their families and friends. *Do you ask for referrals?* No, we don't know how to ask. They just come. *Why don't you run ads about yourselves?* We run ads about our clients' homes. That's what they hire us for. *Do you make cold calls?* No. *Do you call your circle of influence?* Heavens, no. *Do you have a personal brochure?* Never.

The Question

So, this lady in blue was smiling and waiting her turn in the line that formed near the stage after the event. Dozens of audience members wanted to talk one-on-one with the speakers. This woman had been impressed with the panel and was fiercely determined to have her moment with JoAnn.

At last JoAnn finished with the gentleman in front of the lady in the blue suit, and the woman stepped forward. She was in her early 40s, perfectly made up, and she explained that she had been in real estate for almost 20 years. Then this vision in blue asked her question. "Tell me," she said, "what's the one thing you feel is the secret for your fabulous success in so short a time?"

We weren't used to terms like *fabulous*. We just felt lucky. We had no clue how we compared to other agents in the Scottsdale and Phoenix market area, because you couldn't access the data back then. We knew who the local legends were and had completed transactions with a couple of them, but we had no idea that over the previous 12 months we had sold more homes than any other agent in Arizona.

JoAnn seemed not to notice the praise and immediately launched into an explanation of all the things we did to take care of our clients. She told the lady in blue that we put our *clients first* at all times, thus making them feel that to us they are the most important people in the world.

This nice woman waited patiently through it all. She took care to nod at all the correct moments. Then, when JoAnn had finished, with urgency in her voice, she said, "Yes, yes, I understand all that, but tell me, what is the *real* reason for your success?"

It Was Our Fault

Didn't she *get it*? I think if she had, she would have been the one standing on the stage instead of us. She was better dressed. She had worked at least 17 more years in the business. She seemed ambitious and determined. But she just didn't *get it*.

This lovely, well-intentioned woman had been searching for years, her lifetime perhaps, for the secret that would make her a success. We've met thousands of seekers since that day at the Mustang Library, and they all asked the same what-is-the-secret-of-your-success question, and they all dismissed our take-care-of-the-client answer. Were they not listening? No. It was our fault.

We hadn't found a way to explain that real reason. Our answer seemed too simple, too obvious. We didn't have charts or a pyramid diagram or a list of rules. We talked about taking care of clients, and people would say, "Oh, we already do that." Or they would ask, "Is that some kind of customer service thing?" We knew even then that *Clients First* was a two word miracle that, once understood, had the power to change peoples' lives, to transform businesses, and to bring about financial security. We just could not explain it.

For the first half of our lives, we had been just like the blue-suited woman who persevered in her stylish attire. We were fellow travelers. We had struggled with the same question and were left wanting for an answer. We looked for the secret as though it were something others knew and kept from us. We didn't discover *Clients First* until we started to work in the real estate business. Even then, were it not for a dark and stormy night three months into our budding real estate careers, we would still be asking, "What is the real secret to success?"

The Quest

This woman's question at the Mustang Library that morning set JoAnn and me searching for an explanation. We had found something profound, something that changed us and changed our lives. Yet we were unable to explain how it worked.

The explanation would be a quest, a marathon. It would come after seven years spent interacting with thousands of clients. We would first sell a seemingly impossible billion dollars—plus worth of homes. We would live through the greatest real estate bubble and bust in many generations, and we would survive because of something we named *Clients First*. The answer did not come easily. But when it arrived, it came in a moment of inspiration.

If you have been searching, come along as we seek to unlock closed doors and find a path to immense rewards. You will discover open secrets so hidden that they may as well be buried on a distant shore. You will realize that you don't know what you think you know and that you know more than you think. You will find answers within yourself, and you will know that you can achieve great success, because, as you come to know us and our story, you will realize how ordinary we are and how extraordinary has been our experience. An experience you can share and use as your springboard to wealth.

This is the promise of *Clients First*. It will change you. It will change your future. It will last the rest of your life.

In the pages to come, you will learn that nothing is impossible and that everything is possible for you.

But first we must take our journey. We must search for *Clients First*. We must travel southbound on Interstate 84.

2 Road Trip

"**O**h my God, it looks like a war zone." JoAnn looked at a man holding an automatic weapon at his side. "There's another one," she said.

I glanced as she pointed, but I had to keep an eye on the airport traffic. I couldn't tell whether it was Boston SWAT or the Massachusetts National Guard, but there was a trooper every 10 feet along the curb.

"We're not doing this," JoAnn said, shaking her head slowly from side to side. It was the slow part that told me not to argue.

"I'm sure it'll be okay," I said. I knew better, but I can be less than smart when JoAnn shakes her head like that.

We were in Boston for a conference, a gathering of what was billed as the top real estate agents in the country. We were departing with mixed emotions. The presenters had been inspirational, and the people we met were obviously very successful, yet something was missing, and we had been trying to put our fingers on it.

The speakers all seemed to espouse some grand plan or method to achieve success. Our plan seemed so simple, our method so plain. Over the past six years, we had attended dozens of these events all around the country. With each conference, we learned and gained insight, but none provided any great revelations. With each gathering, we came to realize that we did much more business than these high-profile personalities. With each trip we came to realize that our contemporaries were just like our lady in the blue suit. For all their tireless, sincere, and heartfelt efforts, for all their fanciful promotion of their niche secrets to success, they all struggled on, condemned to a business that was only as strong as their next workday. For all their declarations of fundamental truths, we eventually realized that the pronouncements changed like the styles of kitchen cabinets. This was in. That was out. This came back. These experts, these *eagles*, were searching for the real secret and had no idea what it was.

To a person, they made no mention of the client. They had no regard for the most important element in every transaction. How was it that our business success was greater than that of anyone else in the room?

It was during the last day of the conference when news came that British intelligence had thwarted the biggest planned terrorist attack since 9/11. The plot was for suicide zealots to board a dozen or so commercial airliners in London bound for major US cities, including Boston. These Islamic terrorists planned to carry liquid bombs disguised as everyday items, such as shampoo, mouthwash, and soft drinks. They wanted to blow up these planes as they came in for landings on US soil. Not knowing the full extent of the plan, our country was on high alert.

We were scheduled to depart from Boston, and JoAnn wasn't having any of it. "Just keep driving," she said.

"Why?" I said, as JoAnn kept shaking her head. I drove on, protesting as I did. She said something about how I never listen to her—again, a signal that I should acquiesce. I continued by saying that it would surely be safe now: "Just look at all the security."

An hour later, we were back at the Four Seasons, making calls to Amtrak agents, who could get us home in five days—if we didn't mind getting off the train in Flagstaff, which is located 139 miles north of Phoenix. We called our air carrier to change our departure city and learned that Philadelphia, New York, and Washington, DC, were all under alert and, with the disruption in flight schedules, no seats were available. We called our rental car company and inquired about a one-way rental to Phoenix, but neither of us wanted to drive 3,000 miles. We finally came up with Charlotte, North Carolina. The airline had vacant seats, and JoAnn said she would be okay with that.

She also said something about the South being too genteel to be a target. This time, I shook *my* head.

Our decision made, we informed the rental car company, which switched us to a Lincoln Town Car. We bought a road atlas at a bookstore and found the freeway out of town. We ate dinner in Hartford, Connecticut, and drove passed Mark Twain's house while trying to find our way back to Interstate 84.

Was Marketing Our Secret?

Until her cell phone battery ran down, JoAnn spoke to everyone back at our office, trying to plug any leaks in the dike. We hadn't yet made the transition from working *in* the business to working *on* the business, so whenever we were out of town we spent lots of time talking on the phone.

We stopped for the night at a Marriott Courtyard in Hershey, Pennsylvania, and the next morning, while looking for our on-ramp, we passed a Harley-Davidson store with a message-style billboard sign that the owner could change regularly. It read, "If your career is on the rise, put a Harley between your thighs." We discussed this for the next 30 miles.

JoAnn questioned whether the message might be offensive. I thought it was hilarious. From our limited knowledge of the motorcycle industry and biking in general, we tossed our thoughts back and forth. Ultimately, we decided that if Harleys primarily sell to upwardly mobile professionals who like to pretend to be raunchy bikers on weekends, then the sign made an intimate connection with the company's potential customers while disregarding those to whom the lewd connotation might be offensive.

That led us to discuss our own marketing. We had always felt we owed it to our sellers to maximize their homes' exposure with advertising, and we advertised regularly. From day one, we had run ads in the *Arizona Republic* newspaper. I remember telling Sandy, our rep at the paper, that we planned to advertise every week without fail. We'd had our licenses about a month and didn't have any listings yet. Sandy later shared with us that at the time she thought we were crazy. She felt lucky to book a couple ads a week out of our broker's office, and there were more than 100 agents working there.

What bothered us about the conference was that every speaker, every writer, promoter, expert, and agent extraordinaire in attendance seemed to have his or her own version of success and how to achieve it. Was *marketing* the secret to our success? Certainly, many of our clients would say the reason they worked with Those Callaways was because of the advertising. Other agents, if asked, would probably say we were successful because of our marketing.

We drove the next several hundred miles discussing the conference, our business, and our struggle to explain what it was that set us apart. This was August of 2006, and we hadn't taken any real time off in nine years. Now we were traveling south with nothing to do but talk. We were encapsulated in our Town Car and distanced from the daily grind. We had just been to this conference, and it all came pouring out.

Lots of Agents Outspent Us

We had just come through a remarkable period. The market had peaked in 2005. Those Callaways sold over $250 million worth of real estate in that one year alone—more than 500 homes—and we did it one client at a time.

We asked each other what was missing at this conference of industry leaders. We had rubbed shoulders with the best of the best, yet we came away with questions instead of answers.

We continued talking about marketing, but there were countless examples of agents who outspent us. There were agents who couldn't make enough money to pay for their advertising habit. They put their names and their faces everywhere. Whatever they earned they plowed back into marketing in hopes that someday they would make a profit. They feared if they stopped advertising, their businesses would be thrown into tailspins. These agents chased the business, and, although JoAnn and I didn't know it then, they would suffer huge losses when the market later turned downward. It was a lesson we had learned years before. You cannot buy business. The price all too often and all too quickly exceeds the return. Yes, we advertised regularly, but we always kept our marketing expenditures to a percentage of our business volume.

Our ads were beautiful, sincere, and clever, but we didn't have the market cornered on cute. There were plenty of agents with imagination, and the ones without creative genes could copy others. Nobody owns ideas unless he or she spends money to protect them. Then, too, somebody usually thinks of a way to produce knockoffs of the most appealing ads. We always tried to be original and fresh, but there were lots of great ads without our name on them. Just look at that Harley dealer.

Marketing was not our secret any more than it was anybody else's secret. Advertising is something you do to get a little more business, but it's not a success secret. Advertising is just what everybody does. There are no new ideas in marketing. The best you can hope for is to be first with a new twist on an old standard and, when that idea becomes stale from overexposure, try to have the next one ready.

"All these supposedly successful people have their pet themes," I said. JoAnn looked at me knowing I was about to blow off steam. She waited.

"Bob, who everybody agrees is a genius, says that if you spend three hours a day making cold calls on the phone, your business will go through the roof, but he doesn't address what to do with the business after you hang up the phone.

"Then there are a number of agents who teach that all you have to do is ask for referrals on every letter or at the end of every conversation, as if that were some kind of miracle. But no one says what to do with those referrals."

JoAnn said, "We never ask for referrals."

"That's not the point," I said.

"I know," she said, "but we've never made a cold call or asked for a referral."

"I'm talking about how all these guys address just one piece of the puzzle. They all have their own little ax to grind, but no one addresses the heart of the business. What do you do with those clients once you get them?"

I looked over at JoAnn, and she smiled. She got my point. She just liked to throw me off. She was way ahead of me. She was trying to figure it out, too.

What was our secret? Why were we succeeding while not doing any of the things these smart people said to do? What was the answer to the question we'd been asked at the Mustang Library by the lady in blue? We seemed no closer today than we were back then.

Our answer would come, as it always did, in a flash of inspiration two days and 841 miles later.

3 Harper's Restaurant

We sat in a booth by a window facing south with a view of the parking lot and Fairview Road beyond. Our flight wasn't until the next morning, and we had spent the day driving around Charlotte neighborhoods, gawking at houses. The conversation was about business. That's all we ever talked about.

"Do you think we're boring?" I asked.

"No," JoAnn said. "I think we're exciting."

I watched her absorb her environment. She befriended the waitress with a glance. She smiled at me and my heart lost a millisecond. Yes, we are.

"How?" I asked.

"In every way," she said.

"We while away the day. We find a shopping mall. We go to a bookstore," I replied.

"So now you don't like books?" she said.

"No. We're just so predictable."

Our server arrived and we ordered. JoAnn wanted Southern-style veggies and ordered several sides. I had a cheeseburger. Harper's Restaurant sat on a perimeter pad between the shopping center and the busy road. We'd spotted it when we left the Barnes & Noble store where we had just spent an hour browsing in our usual departments: new fiction, mystery, romance, and business, where I found nothing new—or at least nothing I hadn't already purchased sometime in the past 10 years. As our business grew, I constantly sought out the latest how-to-succeed guru. I was that lady in blue at the Mustang Library asking, "What's the *real* secret?" Like everyone else, I hoped for some supreme being in the form of an author to part the heavens and anoint me with the golden wisdom of wealth. But there were no new bibles of business truth today.

It's a Book, It's Not a Book

"Okay," she said, "what's this about?"
"I'm just saying we always do the same things."
"You don't like what we do?"
"I love what we do."
"I know what it is," she said.
"There is no *it*. It's nothing."
"It's the book."
"What book?"
"The book."
"You mean nonbook," I said. "All we have is a file full of notes."
"That's exciting."
"It's not a book," I said.

We had been struggling with this for more than three years, and this road trip had brought my frustration to a peak. We now realized how unique our real estate experiences had been. Our broker, other top agents, first from our state and then from all over the country, had told us our journey was amazing. We'd made more than $200,000 in commissions in our first six months in real estate. This was unheard of. More than 95 percent of agents still in the business felt lucky to make half that each year—and then only after a few lean years. Most agents never make it through the lean years.

We'd hit the ground running and experienced a stellar climb from there. We simply credited it to our hunger for cash. That first half year in the business we seemed to know nothing. We viewed all the big names in our market as legends, with years in the business and signs in front of mansions. They had reputations. We had residents living in a one-square-mile area containing 900 modest homes. We sent cute items to them on a regular basis. Little did we know that we were doing so much more business than these highly touted agents.

In our second year we doubled our income, and in year three we hit $1 million in commissions. That's when people started telling us we were doing well. We had no idea. In 2005, we did almost $6 million in gross commission income. We no longer owed my dad money. In fact, we didn't owe anyone money. We had paid for our home. We had paid for our office. Our retirement was funded. By most measurements, we could pack it in and enjoy our golden years. But here we sat, wanting to tell our story, wanting to explain the reason for our success, yet with no clue how to do it.

The book file was full of stories, systems, tips, and anecdotes. We had outlines and chapter titles, and it was a mess.

JoAnn said, "Let's talk about it."

I pulled out a white 8½ × 11 legal pad. "The problem is I don't know where to begin," I said. "It's, like, too much. It's information overload. And it comes off preachy."

"Well, we certainly don't want to be preachy." She was teasing and I knew it.

"I'm serious."

"Okay, as long as you don't take yourself seriously."

She was right. JoAnn is always right. The book was a gauntlet, a blank page, and I didn't know how to fill it. Every week I wrote ads, letters, flyers, copy for the Multiple Listing Service, tutorials, contracts, counteroffers, addendums, and myriad notes in the course of running our business. But how do you write a book? What was the hook, the main point, the sequence? Who was our audience? There were more than a million real estate agents, but how many would want to know how we did what we did? How many would want to do what we do? How many would even buy a book?

"Who would even want it?" I said.

"Everyone," she replied. "Everyone will want it."

I decided to include a chapter on inspiration and blind adulation.

I wanted this to be more than a real estate book. I wanted this to be the book I had been searching for. I wanted this book to reveal the *real* reason for success. For all of our achievements, for all of our confidence and, yes, for our collective ego (suppressed though it was), I was overwhelmed.

A Working Title

"Let's list the chapters," she suggested.

"We've done that."

"Let's do it again, right now. No notes. Just start with a blank pad."

So we began. I wrote: "Title," followed by the words "*Master Agents, Making Millions Selling Real Estate.*"

"That sucks," she said.

"It's a working title."

"Well, it's not working."

"Can we just get past the first line?"

I started writing chapter titles. "Marketing," "Teaming Up," "Putting Clients First," "Farming," "Systems," "The Internet." We discussed each one as I wrote them down. The waitress poured my third cup of coffee. JoAnn asked for more ice in her tea.

JoAnn examined the page as I looked out the window.

"This is all so good," she said. She read the list aloud. "It's so good."

"It's too much," I said. "It's too general."

"Putting clients first isn't too general. It's important."

"Sure, but everyone preaches good customer service."

"It's more than that," she said. "Putting clients first is much more than good customer service. It's what has made the difference for us. It's what nobody seems to understand."

"So why don't we just call it *Clients First*?"

The minute I said it, we looked at each other. There was no flash of light, but we knew. We felt it. This was our title, our story, our mission.

It Is Instantaneous

This is how so many things happen in our lives, moments of change. Some might call it inspiration or realization, but I call it *change*, because that's what happens. One moment you're going along with your life and then something happens and you change. It is instantaneous. I tried to quit smoking for more than 10 years. I cut down. I changed brands. I bought a pack at a time because a carton was a commitment. Then one night I stopped with half a pack to go. I carried that half pack for months, then kept it in a dresser drawer for years, but I never smoked another cigarette. To this day, I don't know what happened, but I know it happened in a flash and I was changed.

I knew a fellow named Keith who committed to run a marathon. He trained off and on for a few years, and then he got serious and entered a few five-kilometer races and then a half marathon. He trained harder and harder, putting in 50, 60, 70 miles a week. He was totally addicted. Finally, he entered a marathon and ran the whole way. Right after the race a supporter asked Keith what was next and he replied, "I don't care if I never run again." And he didn't. He just stopped. A year later he was asked what happened to him, but he didn't have an explanation. He hadn't thought about it during all the training runs. He didn't plan it. It just happened, and the minute he said it, he was changed. Now we had our title, our moment, and we changed as well.

This book wasn't going to be only about real estate. This was about every business at every level and in every situation. This was what we had been telling everyone for years. This was the elusive secret right out there for anyone to see, and everyone was ignoring it. It was an open secret. No one understood it. No one gave it a second thought. Yet here we were, the perfect ones to explain *Clients First*.

Clueless

I had no idea of the anguish to come. In a moment of change, we had our title, and we had our goal, and we knew it was as right and true as a fair maiden's heart. We just knew that those two words were the secret, the real secret to our success, that they embodied what we did differently from what we had done all those years before when we searched in vain for success and financial security. We knew, but we still we had no idea how to explain *Clients First*.

This would become our greatest challenge. Although we knew in our bones that this was a monumental game changer, we would come to find ourselves mired in the quest to unlock this secret to succeeding in any business. Later, as the months rolled by, we found ourselves just as clueless as all those people who had asked us over the years, "How do you put *Clients First*?"

But at that jubilant moment in Harper's Restaurant in Charlotte, North Carolina, we had no idea of the struggles to come. We were elated. We spoke of little else all the way home. It was all so obvious. This would be easy.

The next morning, we found the Charlotte airport, returned our rental car, and boarded our flight for Phoenix. We weren't even asked for identification. JoAnn was right. The South was too genteel.

On the flight home, we returned to when *Clients First* began. We knew when it happened. We knew the moment we changed for the first time. The challenge would be to explain it. I couldn't explain why I stopped smoking, any more than Keith could explain why he stopped running. And now we had to explain *Clients First*. It would become the hardest thing we ever did.

But we did find the answers. We did unlock the secret to our success. And we can explain it now. To do so, we must go back to that transformational moment. We must go back to a dark and stormy night.

4 A Dark and Stormy Night

"What was that?" I asked.

"You mean about the counteroffer?"

"No," I said, "before that, about keeping the client."

We were driving north on 71st Street, and I remember it as vividly as when Kennedy was shot or when the second tower of the World Trade Center crumbled. It was August, the monsoon season, when the dry heat turns wet. There was lightning, but only a hint of rain. You could smell it. It was past ten o'clock, and this was our second trip to the Smiths' house. We had just left the Browns, and things were not going well.

We had negotiated only a dozen or so deals. We were just getting started, and we were so green. If there was a mistake to be made or a screwup lurking in a corner, we seemed determined to find it. We were intense. We were broke. Well, less than broke. We owed a lot. We even owed my dad, which was sort of the barometer of "brokedom." When we owed Dad, we were there.

I was 50 years old. We hadn't always been broke. We'd had some successes and some failures, some ups and downs. When we started in real estate, we were ending a long hiatus, which some would call a period of not working and spending what we had until there wasn't anything left. Actually, we had spent the past couple of years scouting for books. Every Friday morning we would get up at 4:00 AM to scour the newspaper's classifieds and route our morning. We went to as many yard sales as we could until the sun and heat chased everyone inside. We spent the afternoons going through *our finds* and looking up books in our directories. It was a joyful time for JoAnn and me. Saturday and Sunday were spent doing more of the same, and then throughout the week we went to book dealers, trading our treasures for cash or credit. We had amassed in excess of 10,000 books in our personal collection and made a little money. A little money is defined here as less than it took to live, so we were in debt and needed every deal.

Up to now we had managed to force things. If we got a contract signed and into escrow, it was going to close. Whatever the problem, we found a solution. We knew exactly how much commission was coming, and we had it spent in advance.

I remember the first time we had to give up a piece of the commission because of a discrepancy in the square footage of a house. It was like our fifth deal, and the appraiser came up 200 square feet short. Well, the buyer wanted an adjustment, and our sellers wanted what they thought they had coming; so it became *our* problem. The other agent split the discount with us, and suddenly we had less money than we expected. JoAnn was philosophical about it. I went to bed for a day.

Now we were taking counteroffer number six back to our sellers, the Smiths, and it wasn't really what they needed. The Smiths had already found the house they wanted and had signed a contingent contract to buy it. That meant two deals for us if we could get this deal done. Our buyers, the Browns, had fallen in love with the Smiths' house, but they couldn't afford it. This was 1997, so financing was still a matter of qualifying for a loan and having the job and credit history to pay for what you bought. We knew the Browns would need to sell their house as well, so that was another potential listing and sale.

We were where so many real estate agents find themselves. We were attached to the outcome on so many levels. We had fiduciary obligations to both parties. Arizona is a state that allows *dual agency*, which means you can represent both the buyer and the seller in a transaction. You are held to a higher standard in these situations, but it is possible to serve both sides as long as you are careful about what you disclose and let the negotiation proceed strictly according to what each party says they want to do.

We liked both parties. The Browns were a charming couple. The husband was a jeweler, and his wife was a "Christmas crazy," like JoAnn. The Smiths had four children, including twin toddlers. Here we were, going back and forth, and each step of the way, at some point either the Smiths or the Browns would ask, "What do you think?"

What do you say? How could we be impartial? We knew these people. We liked them. We needed the deal.

Keep the Clients

That's when I asked JoAnn to repeat what she had just said.

She said, "Maybe we should undo it all. We'll find the Smiths another buyer, and we'll find the Browns another house. What matters is that we keep the clients."

There it was.

We both remember it so well and so indelibly. That was the solution. It didn't matter that we had shown the buyers 30 or more houses or that we had held five open houses at the 71st Street home. It was the right thing to do—because it was the right thing to do for our jeweler and the right thing to do for those twins. And that is what we did.

We waited for the inevitable question and when Mr. Smith asked what we thought, we told him the truth as we saw it. We told him we could go to the seller's agent for the house they wanted to buy and ask for an extension. It was a risk, but they needed to hold out for a buyer willing to pay their price. He was relieved. I think his wife started to cry, although she covered it up. The Smiths explained that they had hardly slept for three nights.

When we told the Browns that their counteroffer had been rejected, I believe the same relief was there, but they acted disappointed.

JoAnn assured them we would find another house for them, and when we left it was almost midnight with no moon in the sky and a drizzle in the air.

Nothing Else Mattered

JoAnn and I were changed forever. We never again thought about the commission. We never again begrudged the hours of futility when a home didn't sell for what the sellers wanted or when buyers couldn't find what they had to have. We never again brooded over the expenses on an individual property. We simply knew that as long as we kept the client nothing else mattered. As long as the client's needs came first, we would be rewarded in the satisfaction that we were doing the right thing.

This was the beginning of *Clients First*.

At the time, JoAnn and I knew we were changed by this decision, but what we didn't realize then was that everything and everybody around us would be changed as well. We had no idea that something so simple would have the power to elevate our business, that *Clients First* would attract more clients in more ways than we would ever dream. We had no idea that *Clients First* was contagious and had the power to change others. We had no idea that what had begun as a moment of change would grow into a miracle. We had no idea that this change was only a beginning, only the start of successive changes. We had no idea how big *Clients First* would become in our lives and the lives of others.

What about the Smiths and the Browns? Almost like a fairy tale, although this is a true account, we found a home for the Browns, and they loved it more than the first house. And we did sell the 71st Street home for more money only a week later. *And they all lived happily ever after*.

This simple idea of keeping the client, no matter what—taking care of the client, putting the client first, and thinking only of what was best for this person or that couple—was just an acorn from which a mighty *Clients First* oak would grow. Our business was transformed, and we were transformed. We didn't yet know this would happen. We made only this small change, a commitment that would grow larger in our lives than anything before or since. It would be many years before we realized the enormity of the event. It would take years of struggle to explain it. But this was the beginning. This was the first change.

The next change was not in us but in another person. As striking as was the realization we came to that night, it was dwarfed by what happened the following morning.

5 The Morning After

JoAnn was so eager to tell our two assistants, she hardly slept. She was up and down several times, while I barely moved a muscle. I've always been like that, getting by fine on six or seven hours. JoAnn likes naps.

Marta arrived promptly at 8:30 AM and Susan about 10 minutes later. We felt so fortunate to have found these two women. Or maybe they found us. Marta was one of our earliest clients, and while her house was in escrow she showed JoAnn some flyers she had designed. The ideas were sweet, but what really captured JoAnn's interest was how precise Marta had been when committing everything to paper. Her attention to detail was remarkable.

Marta completed real estate school in less than a month, and we immediately tried to give her the role of transaction coordinator, because we now had several people whose homes were in escrow, and those tasks were time consuming. We needed to be showing and listing homes, not sitting through home inspections and meeting with appraisers. If we didn't like the escrow process, that went double for Marta. She hated it. That's when Susan found us.

Susan, newly licensed, bravely introduced herself one morning at our broker's office. We were dropping off paperwork and picking up mail when she stuck out her hand and told us how much she had heard about us. We were so flattered. She was from Wisconsin, and she was struggling. Susan had just had her first listing appointment the night before, and when the people wouldn't accept her price she turned down the listing. That was so unlike us.

Going against the Current

JoAnn and I would take any listing and then try to make it sell. In fact, though we had already sold several other listings, we still hadn't sold our first listing on Sweetwater Avenue. The home was so overpriced that it would be several months more before we finally sold it. If I had to credit anything for our early success, it would be our dogged determination to make things work. In fact, we can directly credit a dozen good clients we have today to meeting them at that Sweetwater house, which we held open week after week.

We did a lot of that back then, going against the current wisdom. I remember thinking at the time, Susan's decision to turn down those potential clients was foolish, but she had that spark in her eye and a wholesomeness that could only be grown in small-town America. She was just doing what they taught in real estate class. We were a bit more independent.

Susan had recently earned a degree in music and could play every instrument in a symphony orchestra. We knew she was special and hired her immediately, putting her to work on escrows. Marta almost cried with relief.

As excited as we were from the revelation of the night before, there was no time to talk all morning. I was busy at the computer, lining up houses to show to the client we were meeting in the afternoon. Marta was preparing the weekend's classified ads for the open house directory. Susan had two inspection reports to oversee and a buyer's request for repairs. JoAnn was at our kitchen booth still making notes on our Today List, in between originating and receiving phone calls, which was a challenge because we only had one phone. It was a Princess model with a 50-foot cord. It had a call-waiting feature that gave us two lines, and we held it to our ear so we didn't miss a call as we passed it back and forth from the dining room to the kitchen to the living room.

Group Therapy

Finally, JoAnn couldn't wait any longer, and she told Marta to set the chairs in a circle between the dining room and the living room and to bring the phone. This was unusual. It was probably our first such meeting, and I think it worried Marta and Susan a little.

JoAnn had told me what she wanted to do that morning as we dressed. I said, "Sure," but I said sure to almost anything JoAnn said. Let's go rob a bank. Sure. Let's have another child. Well, almost anything.

Marta and Susan moved their chairs about five feet, and I brought the two chairs from our desks. We didn't have a couch, so there was plenty of room, and we all sat down like folks do at a group therapy session. Susan was all smiles. Marta was flushed. JoAnn didn't want to alarm them, so she said, "This is something good."

JoAnn told them about the night before. She filled them in on the last two counteroffers. They both pretty much knew about the offer and the first few counteroffers. This had been going on for days. They also knew the Smiths and the Browns from listening to us talk and listening to JoAnn's phone calls. Ours was a very open environment.

When JoAnn got to the part about finding our buyer another house and finding our seller another buyer, I half worried that they would be disappointed. This would mean more work for us—and being paid later, if at all. It was a risk.

I think Susan saw the rightness of the concept, but she was very competitive and hated to lose. I think she may have felt that this was like losing. She was young, twentysomething, and frustration showed on her forehead as three horizontal furrows. "I know we'll keep the seller. We have a listing," she said. "But we could lose our buyer over this."

"Yes," JoAnn said.

"Well, that sucks."

"Yes," JoAnn said, "but we'll just have to work hard to find them another house and hope they will stick with us."

"For that matter," I said, "we could lose our seller, too." I thought Susan blanched a little.

"Look," JoAnn said, "it's the right thing to do, and it's what we are going to do from now on. All we are going to care about is keeping the client by doing what's best for the client."

Susan smiled her sweet smile and nodded. It was Susan's basic goodness that first attracted us. Her heart knew we were right—even if it meant a delay in receiving her money. I knew she had her own little record of what we had in escrow and when they were supposed to close. The money was very important to her.

The Right Thing to Do

Marta hadn't said anything, so JoAnn asked her what she was thinking. I'll never forget her initial reaction.

"I'm glad," she said. "It really wasn't the best thing for either of them."

That was it. Marta was not one to mince words or to waste them. Marta saw it immediately and, like us, was forever changed. She knew that it was more than the right thing to do. She recognized the power of what we were saying. She knew this was a transformational moment for her as well.

Marta was from Chicago and had worked all her life, mostly in office jobs for small companies. She had served as a gal Friday, and often it was just Marta and the owner working together in a room. She had watched what owners worried about and how they set their priorities. Months later, she told us that about the only time these businesspeople cared about the customers was when there was a complaint to resolve—and that even then they seldom strayed from what was best for them. She told us that one man she'd worked for in Chicago actually said that customers were a necessary evil.

But on this day she had little to say, just that it was the right thing to do. It wasn't until a week or two later that I realized how much of an impact this had made on Marta. It became a part of her daily language. In almost every situation, she started asking what was best for the client. She became our reminder. She believed it to her core, and she infected all of us.

Susan accepted a position as a music director a few months later, but Marta was with us for another eight years. When Marta returned to Chicago to care for her mother, she continued to work for us from her home, but we had to replace her in the office. Marta was the heart of our business, and finding her replacement was easy because she has left us with an office filled with hearts as pure as hers. It was Marta's influence that shaped so many on our great team.

That morning, we learned that this was more than a powerful concept. This was an idea that could be immediately conveyed and could change others. First, we were changed; then Marta was changed. You, too, can be changed. This miracle is something that can be passed on and shared.

A Two Word Mission

We didn't call it *Clients First* back then. That would come three years later. We simply expressed it as nothing else matters as long as we do what is best for the client. Money didn't matter. The possibility of the client dropping us and going elsewhere didn't matter. If we screwed up or made an embarrassing mistake, it didn't matter. All that mattered was keeping the clients by doing what was best for them.

Eventually we embodied the concept in two words: *Clients First*. We called it our two word mission statement and put it on our website and in our marketing materials in 2001. We told new team members and watched as it transformed them. Unabashed at the simplicity of the promise we made, we told clients. Yes, we told the lady in blue that morning at the Mustang Library and the top agents we met around the country, but it seldom had an impact.

Perhaps it was working with JoAnn and me each day that changed our team. Maybe the clients took it with a grain of salt, although I believe some were deeply moved by our sincerity. We expressed it at every turn, and when people asked how you put *Clients First*, we would talk on and on, obviously failing from the looks in their eyes. We simply could not explain it, because, although it had changed our lives, the answer was just beyond our reach, waiting for us to change again.

It would be years later, more than two years after our conversation in Harper's Restaurant in Charlotte, North Carolina, before we could explain the *how*. How do you put *Clients First*? What do you do? The answer would come. The answer came when we discovered the three keys.

6 The Three Keys

We knew the explanation of *Clients First* had to be simple. There had to be a way to reveal the secret to our success. We knew we had been transformed that night so many years ago. The change came in an instant. We knew that Marta the next morning, then Susan in the weeks following, and then our staff over the years had all been deeply affected as well. But how could we share this with other people who didn't work with us every day? How could we answer the question, "What do you do to make *Clients First*? It was as if the explanation were in a locked magic room for which we had no key. If only we could find a way to relate *Clients First*.

People Are Not Changed

In my first attempt to put pen to paper after our experience in Charlotte, I wrote down a list of 122 ways to put clients first. I did this in a flash of inspiration at two o'clock in the morning. The next day, JoAnn read my list and said, "I didn't know you had it in you."

"What?" I said, "You think you're the only one who takes care of the clients?"

It wasn't going well.

Although it was a good list, it wasn't new or unique. The essence of my list existed in dozens of books, newsletters, magazines, and newspaper articles. It was just another version of the same customer service stuff people have been reading for years. While each item was valid and rang true, how could we expect people to remember it all? How could we expect this to change anyone? It was like one big to-do list: *Do this. Get inspired about that.* In the end, people are not changed. This would just exhaust a person and ultimately be forgotten.

For the next year or so, we talked about it off and on. Actually, I had begun to grumble. JoAnn remained positive, but neither of us could unlock the magic room. We were searching for *Clients First.* We talked to each other and we talked to people we knew. We talked to staff. We talked to other agents with whom we had professional relationships. We talked to vendors and mortgage people and title officers. We talked to everybody. We tested this theory and that theory. We received a lot of wonderful comments about taking care of clients, but these were just another 122 ways to please clients. *Send them handwritten notes. Smile. Use first names.* I wanted to scream.

Clients Last

This was impossible. I reread all the books. We bought new ones. Nothing. *Clients First* had become a grueling quest, a confused quagmire of *sucking up.* There is nothing worse than *sucking up.* It's phony. I love it when a server with a soprano voice asks, in an alto voice, if she can take our order. This two-octave change in tone tells me she is faking it; when she brings me cream with my black coffee, I know she hasn't been listening.

I got so bogged down in bad customer service that I suggested we call it "Clients Last." Thankfully, JoAnn said no. She said there might be a place for the comparison, but only when we could first explain *Clients First.*

It was like looking for something misplaced. It nagged at us. It became a burden. More than once, one of us would ask the other, *"You want to give up? We can forget it. The world doesn't need another book."* No. We would shake our heads. This was something we had to do.

Narrowing It Down

Then one Sunday morning we were having brunch at the Princess Resort. It's called the Scottsdale Fairmont today, but it will always be the Princess to us. I asked JoAnn, "If you had to narrow it down, what 10 things define *Clients First*?"

It was kind of an out-of-the-blue question, because we hadn't really spoken of it for a couple of months. I don't know where the number 10 came from. It could have been a dozen or eight. I just wanted to get away from the list of 122. She thought about it, and as she said each item I wrote them on a scratch pad. We ended up with 11 principles, and it was an excellent list.

The next day, I pulled out the 122-item list, and, sure enough, every item on that long list could be assigned to one of the 11 on the short list. We were on to something, and I thought about it all week.

The next Sunday morning, like a superstitious baseball player, I took JoAnn back to the Princess for brunch. We even waited so we could sit at the same table.

We talked about how much more powerful the short list was. Maybe 11 things could be memorably conveyed. We talked about how maybe we could take the list of 11 items and make it 12, then have each one start with one of the letters in *Clients First* (C for *cooperation*, L for *love*, etc.), but that just sounded contrived.

We talked about change. We talked about how keeping the clients by taking care of them had transformed us. We asked how these things on our list would change a person. That was the key question. That was the standard by which any of the principles or rules or standards or whatever you wanted to call them had to be measured. The key would be change, or transformation. In a moment, on that dark and stormy night all those years ago, we had become different people because we decided to put clients first.

By this measure, our list of 11 was close but, as they say, no cigar. These items didn't require change. They didn't shake a person to the core. They didn't part the clouds and open the heavens.

Scary True

Still, the 11-item list was stronger than a long list. Then I said, "Could we combine any of these?" And that was the moment it changed. In less than 10 minutes we had three keys. In the time it took to drink a second cup of coffee, we had unlocked the door to the magic room.

It was scary. Could it really be this simple? We had three keys and everything fit. All the cylinders in the lock lined up. We could not believe it. Condensing the list of 11 into three keys made the concept a hundred times more powerful. The original 122 principles were all in there. If we made a list of 1,022 or even 1,000,022, it would all come back to these three keys. We were at once elated and frightened.

For the next year, we talked about the three keys. We searched for a possible fourth key. There were runners-up, to be sure, but none were essential. These runners-up were not transformational. They might change a person initially and stay with some people for a long time. But they weren't like the three keys. They weren't scary true.

We asked ourselves what would happen if there are only two keys. We measured each against the other. Each of these keys stood alone in their power to transform, but to remove one would be like removing one leg from a three-legged stool. All you had then was kindling for the fireplace.

For many months, we examined every encounter and measured them all by the three keys. We looked at our team and saw where the three keys were working, and, yes, we saw where they were not at work; when we took steps to implement the three keys, they became powerful problem solvers. At last we knew the secret to *Clients First* and could quantify it. We could answer the question. We could even tell the lady in the blue suit precisely how we put *Clients First*.

A Two Word Miracle

Is this the only secret to success? Probably not, but it was ours. We had lived it and experienced it firsthand. We searched for the explanation, struggled, finally found the answer, and could now explain it.

As the three keys are revealed to you, we hope you will also be changed. *Clients First* is a two word miracle that can be your miracle to trigger an irreversible change. You will be haunted by these three keys and the all-encompassing power they possess. You will measure everything you do by them and will find success flowing to you like a river pouring from a fallen dam.

The three keys come in no set sequence. Each key is important, and each one stands alone. *Clients First* is achieved only when all three keys are used. Imagine *Clients First* as a room behind a door with three deadbolts. You cannot unlock *Clients First* without inserting all three keys.

7

The First Key

That night, the night we struggled to serve both the Smiths and the Browns, when JoAnn said maybe we should undo it all, that all that mattered was that we keep the client, she was talking specifically about that one difficult deal we were trying to make work. Yet what she said spoke much more about who we were, where we were, what we were doing, and how we were doing it.

We were just getting started in the real estate business. We had been at it for four months and had achieved, by most people's standards, early success. Selling houses suited us. It suited our talents. JoAnn was good with people and I was good with paperwork. But it was more than that.

Residential resale is really just a part of the real estate world. It's only a part, but it is where most people start, because it seems easy. In Arizona, you attend 90 hours of classes and take a state exam. You pay your fees to the Arizona Department of Real Estate and the local Association of Realtors. You're interviewed by a couple of brokers, and bam, you're a real estate agent. Then you have to figure out what to do.

We Had Bills to Pay

Our broker, like all good brokers, had a training program for newbies. We attended a few classes, but the instruction didn't fit us. They talked about calling people we knew (*circle of influence*, they called it) and telling them we were in real estate. Beyond our grown daughters and a few service people, JoAnn and I didn't have a circle. Not that we were antisocial, but we tended to keep to ourselves. We lived shy and quiet lives. Our relationship is such that I am JoAnn's best friend and she is mine, which is a blessing, but in the case of starting out in real estate and not having a lot of friends, it could be a curse.

If you didn't have a circle of influence, then the instructor suggested *cold calling*. Just open up the phone book (this was before the Do Not Call Registry), dial random numbers, and start talking to people. We looked around the room at heads nodding and stopped going to classes. Besides, they were talking about making a sale a month, and we needed more than that. We had bills to pay.

Emotional Overflow

We were ambitious and had each other, which in residential resale is a huge advantage, because the emotional toll is heavy. In most businesses, the focus is on the numbers. But when you are selling homes, it is all about emotion. It doesn't matter whether people are buying a home or selling a home (and they are sometimes doing both at the same time), it is usually the biggest financial transaction of their life; they don't do it every day, and their home is an intensely personal possession. Folks get angry; they cry; they experience everything from fear to elation; and through it all, they rely greatly on their real estate agent, who may or may not be up to the task. This was where JoAnn and I did well. We quickly became each other's rock. Whatever the client's emotional overflow, we were able to accept it and keep each other sane.

Where we were was Scottsdale, Arizona. *What* we were doing was selling real estate. *How* we were doing it was with a lot of drive and ambition, shored up by our ability to lean on each other. But when JoAnn said all that mattered was keeping the client, we had to change something. We had to set aside our personal situation and forget about the money. We had to tell the Browns and the Smiths what we really thought. We had to think about what was best for them.

A Hundred Ways to Be Truthful

Even with our limited experience, we still knew more about the situation that night than they did. Our opinion had value. But our opinion could sink the deal. We could lose one or both clients. There were so many other options. We could just let them go along without our input. What did it matter if their decisions were made emotionally, without a full understanding of the facts? We could try to anticipate which way they were leaning and tell them what they wanted to hear. There were a dozen options.

Until that night, these options seemed reasonable, if not prudent. All our lives we'd had options. We always considered ourselves forthright. But there seemed to be a hundred ways to be truthful. Prior to our decision to take care of the client, it had always been possible to rationalize any option we chose.

Now we suddenly had only one option, only one way to reconcile the facts. As much as the Browns loved the Smiths' home, the unemotional truth was that it was more than they could afford. Yes, the loan officer could stretch their qualifications, but how truthful was that? They could have made the purchase, but the house would have owned them. They would have had to make unpleasant cuts in their lifestyle to make the monthly payments.

There was only one option for us when we took that counteroffer to the Smiths. As much as they wanted that next home, which Mrs. Smith had fallen in love with, they were blinded with the fear of losing that next home if they didn't sell their current house quickly. They were going to accept less than they should and less than they needed. They were about to put themselves into the same financial squeeze as the Browns.

Honesty Was the Key

We had only one option if we were to do what was best for these clients: We had to be honest. Even if they didn't ask, which, thankfully, they did, we would have to tell them it was a mistake to go forward. We had to help them to remove the emotion. From now on, this was our job: We were taking care of the client, and that demanded total honesty and one truth as we saw it. That was our value to them.

We told them the truth as we saw it, and that night we were transformed. *Clients First* changed how we dealt with the truth. Honesty was the key, and it changed not only JoAnn and me, it also changed our relationships with our clients, and, ultimately, it changed our clients.

Before *Clients First*, we always thought of ourselves as good people. Sure, JoAnn would tell little white lies to save hurting others. I was very *creative* when necessary. We weren't above covering a mistake now and then as long as it didn't really matter. We both had excellent memories. But that night, when we decided nothing else mattered as long as we kept the client, we suddenly had a different standard by which to measure our success, and toying with the truth did not work anymore.

- How could we put clients first if we were not truthful with them?
- How could they trust us if we weren't willing to trust them with the truth?
- How could anything short of complete honesty ever be justified?

These questions changed everything, and, as JoAnn and I look back, we realize the change was immediate. JoAnn and I didn't start saying out loud that we needed to be truthful. We did talk a lot about how we had to put the client first. In fact, I don't think we ever spoke of honesty. Our truthfulness came about because we could not serve the client any other way.

Honesty Set Us Free

The positive effects of what we told the Smiths and the Browns were almost immediate, but how this changed our business grew gradually, like a snowball rolling downhill.

The first thing we noticed when we put clients first was a new feeling of strength and courage. It was incredibly liberating. By no longer having to juggle the facts, we were relieved of the strain. When you have only the truth, you have no moral dilemmas. You sleep well at night. You don't have to have a good memory. Honesty set us free.

When you are truthful with clients, you know you're doing the right thing. You don't feel as if something was left unsaid or undone. We felt closure, and in the end it made everything easy.

A Fairy-Tale Ending?

Would all of this have happened the same way if we had lost the clients that night? What if the Browns had said, "Fine, there are plenty of agents in the sea, we'll go fish elsewhere"? What if the Smiths had lost the dream home they wanted to buy and had just decided to take their home off the market? What if it hadn't happened like it did, with a fairy-tale ending?

I don't know. Maybe we would have gone on and kept our commitment to putting *Clients First*. Then again, maybe we would have lost heart after a while and gone on to have a real estate career marked with toil and hard work and time spent thinking more about ourselves and how to make ends meet. Maybe we would have had a degree of success without changing. We certainly were driven. I don't know, but what I do know is that JoAnn and I are grateful for the way it happened. We found a new way to look at the truth and a comfort with the truth we didn't have before.

I also know that *Clients First* is imbued with magic. It seems to attract little miracles every day. I don't believe it was just a happy coincidence that caused everything to work out for the Browns and the Smiths. There are forces out there that we do not see. Things happen sometimes because they are supposed to happen. We discovered *Clients First* and then discovered the three keys because it was meant to be.

A Powerful Effect

Part of the reason it worked like a charm is that *Clients First* changed our relationships with clients. We trusted them with the truth, and they trusted us. By being honest, we were saying to them that we believed they deserved the truth and could handle it. *We empowered our clients.*

The Browns stuck with us, in spite of their disappointment, because we told them the truth. The Smiths remained confident in our ability to find another buyer because we told them the truth when they needed to hear it. Putting them first had a powerful effect on the Browns and the Smiths, and they stayed with us.

Insurance

That night, we knew we had done our best and had no regrets. We knew things don't always go right, yet we knew if things went wrong, our clients would know we'd done our best and wouldn't blame us. Honesty was the best insurance we could buy.

The other day, I heard an agent say, "If you haven't been sued, you aren't doing enough business." I thought about that. On the one hand, I was saddened by the expectation it implied and, on the other hand, struck by the notion that litigation is a fact of life. By being honest, your chances of being sued plummet.

Fairness

Our relationship with the Smiths and the Browns changed that night on many levels. Our decision to take care of our clients demanded a new and singular approach to the truth: that we treat them fairly. What was unexpected was that clients treated us fairly in return.

A part of the Realtor Code of Ethics says we are to treat all parties fairly. So much of what we do is about acting in good faith. We trust that people mean what they say and will do what they promise to do. Telling the truth is the only path to that fairness, and when it begins with you, it comes back to you from your clients.

A Powerful Magnet

Our fairness with the Browns and the Smiths gave them confidence. They knew they could rely on us, and they were liberated from doubt and indecision. They knew we were putting their interests first, and they knew we would not betray them.

Our honesty inspired these clients—and thousands since. It became infectious. It became a huge and powerful magnet. These clients were drawn to us. Since that night, nothing has mattered to us except keeping the client. As a consequence, the Browns, the Smiths, and so many clients since have become attached to us.

We found that our truthfulness motivated our clients to tell others. They believed they had found a good thing and wanted to share this discovery with family and friends. Our business grew exponentially and without explanation. We never again prospected. We never even asked for referrals.

JoAnn grew up with her own sense of propriety, and I love her for it. She believes there are some things you just don't do—and one of them is to ask for business. She believes it's in poor taste. My reason was different. I didn't know how to ask for a referral without coming off as a needy jerk. I don't know if that is true for everyone, but it is for us. So we never ask. Simply by putting our clients first, they became an army of recruiters.

For all of the power of honesty it is but the first key. Honesty may liberate you. Honesty may attract clients. But honesty alone is not enough. You need the second key.

8   The Second Key

When JoAnn and I started out in real estate we were as green as grass. We took the classes and passed the state test, but we had no clue about what to do. At a garage sale, I had picked up a book written by a former real estate agent. It was all about picking 500 homes and going door to door with a business card. So I picked a thousand homes and went door to door and came away with little more than juicy gossip.

We took new-agent classes at our broker's office, and the instructor mentioned calling on *expireds*, people whose listing contracts had run their course. I never got past the first one. The gentleman, a former agent as well as the home owner, laughed at me. He said, "I didn't know agents still did this." I went back to my car and drove straight home, where JoAnn was taking a nap. She was always smarter than me.

Yolanda, another agent at our broker's office, told us she worked only with buyers but that she had listed her neighbor's home and that we were welcome to hold the house open on the weekends. The property backed up to the busiest street in Paradise Valley. The backyard was small and the noise deafening. We worked there every weekend, and JoAnn met a few people, but she waited a week to follow up. She thought it improper to call too soon. Most had already found a house. That's when we learned about urgency. When clients want a house, they want it *right now*.

Our First Contract

Yolanda told us she was going on vacation and asked if we would handle her buyers while she was gone. It was for only a week, and we appreciated the opportunity. We said yes, and about halfway through the week, this buyer of hers said he wanted to make an offer on a house he had seen before. We met him at our broker's office and wrote our first contract. It was a disaster.

We didn't know what we were doing, and wherever the contract gave an option for the buyer versus the seller to pay for something, our buyer said to check *seller*. We sent the contract to the seller's agent and got this awful phone call from the agent telling us that her seller was insulted and so was she. She said, "Don't you even know it's customary for the buyers to pay for their own loan costs?"

About that time, Yolanda returned from vacation and *blew up*. JoAnn told her that we did exactly what the buyer told us to do, but now the buyer was saying that he only followed our lead. Yolanda told JoAnn that she didn't know who to believe, and that was the end of our relationship.

We were distraught that we had let down our fellow agent's client. We were appalled at our treatment by the seller's agent. But it was our fault. We were not competent.

Our first listing came from a neighbor. Her name was Toni and she owned a house on Sweetwater. This was shortly after the contract fiasco, and when Toni came to our door, JoAnn said, "Oh, you don't want us, we don't know what we're doing." However, Toni insisted, and we went over to fill out a listing form—but only after a visit to our broker to make sure we didn't do anything stupid.

We listed the house for $38,000 more than it eventually sold for, but Toni never complained when it took seven months to sell. She and her family moved to Oklahoma, and to this day we send client mailings to her. Even from out of state she has sent clients to us. Thank goodness we never made a major mistake in selling her house on Sweetwater.

Seven Days a Week

We sold 16 houses before we closed on the Sweetwater deal, but it was an excellent training ground for us. We held it open every Saturday and Sunday. JoAnn called the clients she had met at the open house on the busy street and invited them to come see the Sweetwater property. We began showing homes. We showed a lot of homes. We worked seven days a week. I spent endless hours on the Multiple Listing Service computer and sometimes worked until two o'clock in the morning. We each had one good pair of jeans. JoAnn washed them overnight, and I ironed creases into them each morning.

We didn't have a cell phone, but a friend named Donna, who later became our first showing agent, was married to a fellow who worked for the electric power company. His company had issued a cell phone to him, and Donna offered it to us on weekends when Lonnie was off. It was shaped like a brick and weighed three pounds, but we were thrilled to have it.

We wrote a lot of offers. This was 1997, and the real estate market was flat. Buyers were initially unrealistic, and we typically wrote five contracts for every one that was accepted. We stopped going to the new-agent classes and concentrated on knowing what we were doing when it came to serving the client. We became competent.

On that night when we sat down with the Smiths and then the Browns, having decided to put these *Clients First* and that nothing else mattered as long as we took care of and kept these clients, we were grateful for our newly developed knowledge and abilities. The lessons up to now were hard earned, and we had made some stupid mistakes, but this night we knew enough. By the next morning, we knew we had to know more; we had to know it all. How could we put our *Clients First* until we were competent?

Competence is the second key. Without competence, you can fail a client in a hundred ways.

Our industry gets a bad rap because of its apparent low entry requirements. There are those who say it takes 2,000 hours to become a hairdresser and only 90 to become a real estate agent. Lawyers and doctors spend years in school. Tradespeople must go through apprenticeships. This is all true, but there comes a moment when the hairdresser cuts that first paying customer's hair, the lawyer makes a first appearance in front of a judge, and the carpenter begins work on a first remodeling project. At that moment, they all question their competence. Education is not enough. Everyone must gain experience.

I remember as a teenager complaining that I couldn't get a job without experience and I couldn't get experience without a job. Eventually, however, I did get an opportunity, and you will, too. When that opportunity comes, it is what we make of it that matters. Choose to know what you are doing or quickly find out what is required. It is only when you are competent that you can best serve your clients, and it is only by best serving your clients that you put them first.

Be the Best

Our decision to put *Clients First* required us to not only know what we were doing but to know how to do it better than anyone else. And because our commitment was so strong, we felt a need to constantly find ways to be more and more competent. *Clients First* compelled us to do better, to be the best.

From that quest to be the best, *Clients First* changed us further. We looked at our practice of real estate with new eyes. How could we possibly put *Clients First* and serve more than one client at a time? After all, a client deserved our full attention. The minute the cell phone rang with a call from a second client, the first client was neglected.

Until this time, real estate agents were a one-person show. They tried to do everything for everybody. Some hired an assistant or two to remain in the background and take care of paperwork, but the agents still handled all the client contact. Many agents still operate this way today. Some work in teams, dividing the client load. When one agent goes on vacation, the other agent acts as a substitute. We knew first-hand how that might fail. We needed a new way to operate if we were going to put *Clients First* and serve more than one client at a time.

We had already hired two assistants with the first model in mind. Marta worked on marketing materials and Susan kept the escrow files in order. Although both were licensed real estate agents, their client contact was limited to answering the phones and placing some calls for JoAnn. We still handled all the client contact. But with *Clients First*, we knew we needed to involve Marta and Susan directly with the clients.

Only One Instruction

Gradually, using baby steps at first, we involved Marta in the listing process. When a "list me" call came in, Marta would talk to the person and ask about his or her situation and set our appointment time. This was a small beginning, but by making it a small part of the process, Marta became very competent. She developed a whole routine. She had her list of questions written down so she wouldn't forget one. She focused on what a new client needs when he or she calls about listing a home. She improved upon how we served that client at that moment in the real estate process. She became better than we were at this, and she did it without supervision and only one instruction: Put the *Client First*.

Marta's story is a powerful one, because it was a test, and she passed with an A-plus. Marta's competence was a key to our success. She demonstrated to us that our competence could not only be multiplied but that it could be improved upon; it could be the best. Actually, JoAnn and Marta would banter back and forth, with Marta saying we should be the biggest and JoAnn saying we should be the best. In the end, the goals merged and we settled on both.

Today we have 30 licensed assistants on our team. Each of them, like Marta, handles a step in the process, and each of them, like Marta, does so without supervision and with only one instruction: Put the *Client First*. Our clients are better served than they would be if JoAnn and I had only one client. The reason they are better served is because the aggregate experience and expertise of 30 agents far exceeds anything we could supply alone.

How do our clients feel about this? They love it. They love it so much that not a day goes by without a call from a new client who was urged to call us by a past client. And yes, JoAnn still thinks it is in poor taste to ask for referrals. They just call. We have clients who know every agent on the team. We have clients who on their first visit to the office will ask, "Now which one is Marti?"

Today's seller, for instance, will talk to Marti, then Joyce, then Ed when he comes out to measure the home. Then she meets Kelly, who guides the client in filling out the paperwork. Then Judy comes out to *stage the home* and Aaron comes to photograph it. Brian arrives to film the virtual tour. All this time, Joyce is scheduling these events and more. Once our seller's home is on the market, she meets Donna, who oversees an open house. When we receive an offer, she talks to JoAnn or me, and when we make a deal, Lupe (who does the job Susan began so long ago) takes over and gets her through inspections and escrow.

Every step of the way, our clients are met with competence. Every step of the process demonstrates that we put our *Clients First*.

Pursue Competence

Today, every contract is still written or reviewed by JoAnn or me. We estimate we have probably handled more than 15,000 contracts over the years, and on every one of them we are reminded of that first fiasco. We still negotiate every deal. We know every client. Because of our team and their competence, we have the time to serve every client personally. We don't use voice mail. If we can't take a call when it comes in, a competent team member speaks to the client and we call the person later. JoAnn's rule is that no call goes unreturned. We can't go home until every client is served.

Over the years, we have sought competence. Every two years we are required to complete 24 hours of continuing education. We estimate the team has attended and completed more than 4,000 hours of instruction. JoAnn and I personally attend from 5 to 10 conventions and seminars each year. We attend two Mastermind lunches each month. We schedule lunches and dinners with other top-producing agents. We hear speakers at the home tour meetings. We read hundreds of e-mails, attend webinars, buy and read books, subscribe to and read all trade magazines, and listen to CDs in the car. We do this to be competent, to be better, and to put our *Clients First.*

Yet honesty and competence are not enough. To truly put *Clients First*, you must have the third key, without which you may as well pack up and go home.

9

The Third Key

Before that night when JoAnn and I decided to put clients first, that nothing else mattered as long as we kept the client, we thought a lot about our situation. We thought about money. With three grown daughters, it was always something. We thought about money. We still had both our parents, and we had issues to deal with there. We thought about money. We thought about our past ups and downs. We thought about money. At 50, we had no savings, no equity in a home, and my dad had financed the car we were driving. We thought about our future financial security. And yes, we thought about money.

We talked about *us*. We talked about our politics, losing weight, what to have for dinner, the books we were reading, religion, family, and money. Even after a lifetime of marriage, we still had fights or spats or whatever you want to call them. Then we would make up, which was the good part. Then we talked some more about money. All our lives we had talked about money, how to get it, how to spend it, and what we would do with it if there were any left over, which there never was.

As Long as We Were Paid

Now we had gotten into real estate, and again we talked about money. Everything we did was immediately equated to commission. This closing could pay these bills. The next could go to those bills. One more, and maybe we could have a cushion. Oh, we were working hard, and if you had asked us, we would have said that were doing a good job for our buyers and sellers—but it was all about the commission. And when we screwed up, which happens when you are new, we were introduced to the "commissionectomy." That's when your commission is reduced to pay for a mistake, such as missing the fact that the house has a septic tank instead of sewer. We had a few of these commission adjustments, but we were proud of the fact that we never had a deal *fall out of escrow*. They all *closed*, because we needed the money and we made sure they did. We actually thought that was a selling point: "List with us and we will *get you closed*." We didn't care what the obstacle might be—we didn't care about anything as long as we were paid.

When you put clients first, it can't be about *your* money, it has to be about *their* money. Again, the realization was instantaneous. In order to put *Clients First* we would stop caring about *us* and we would start caring about *them*.

A New Definition

This is not to say we hadn't always cared about people. But now we had a different definition for caring. We had defined *caring* as sympathy or empathy. When people had troubles, we felt badly for them. I always get extra napkins at the movies because JoAnn and I always cry at the end. I used to complain that one of the reasons we had no money was because we kept giving it away to the kids.

We cared about doing a good job. We felt badly when we made mistakes, and we always resolved to improve ourselves.

We had goals and dreams and wanted to fulfill them. We had wants and needs and worked hard to satisfy them.

But now caring had a new definition. If we were to put our *Clients First*, then we had to care only about them. Their goals and dreams had to become ours. What they wanted or needed became what we wanted or needed. To care about clients was to share their aspirations.

When you put *Clients First*, the conversation is all about them. Everything about you is what you can do for them. The client becomes your obsession. *You are the client.*

When you are the client, you have strength. When you are the client, and the client misleads him- or herself, you have the strength to say so. When you are the client, you know what is best and you say so. When you are the client, you fight for *yourself*. Today, we do everything for our clients. We have only one level of service. *Clients First* demands it. Now, some clients will initially say they want less fuss, but they seldom say it for long. They like the fuss. They like being made to feel that they are our number one priority. They like feeling safe. They like knowing in their hearts that all we want is what's best for them. They know we care, and that is everything.

Every agent on our team is empowered to care. We tell each of them we have a two word mission statement and it is, *"Clients First."* I cannot count how many times a day I hear those two words in conversations that take place at our office. It is a two word miracle, and it is the bottom line that influences all decisions.

It Focused Us

For years, JoAnn and I went on every listing appointment. Our day was one long interruption. We went to seminars where they taught that we had to work *on* our business as much as we worked *in* our business. This was frustrating, because our day consisted of an hour in the office, then leaving to keep an appointment, then returning to the office for half an hour, then leaving for another listing appointment, and then returning for an hour and a half before leaving again. Many days, we had five listing appointments.

How could one possibly juggle all that? We made calls as we traveled in the car. While walking up front walkways, we might be discussing any number of business issues, yet when JoAnn knocked on the door, things changed. When prospective clients opened the door, they became our clients, and we put them first. We cared about their situation, and all else vanished. We walked out of listing appointments, got in the car, and shook our heads, marveling at how we had thought of nothing else while in that home except the clients' needs.

Best Serve Their Interests

Caring and putting *Clients First* is something we encourage, nurture, and protect every day. Every conversation with a client is about his or her specific needs. One of my favorite openings is, "Tell me about your situation." I have had clients remark that I was the first person to show concern. Can you imagine? I was the first person to ask about them. We ask, and then we ask some more. Some people are open books, and some folks are like onions, with layer after layer that needs to be peeled away. Often, people are dealing with emotional issues, family problems, embarrassment, or despair. Some clients' walls or shields are penetrated only when they realize you care. Caring promotes sharing, and only when we understand their situations are we able to best serve their interests.

Every day we tell our clients that we care, but we seldom say it outright. We demonstrate it with our actions and by how we deal with questions and issues. We tell them that we have a two word mission statement and that it is *Clients First*. When they have a decision to make, we remind them that all we care about is what is best for them. Clients often ask for our opinions or input, and when we offer it, we always put it in the context of what we think is the best decision for them. We make their goals our goals, and we do everything possible to achieve those goals. That is our job.

The Power of Caring

JoAnn and I are great believers in the law of attraction. This principle says we get what we believe we will get, that we attract what is in our thoughts. By caring about our clients, their goals become our goals. We believe in their goals and believe we will achieve them. We attract positive results for our clients.

Because we care about our clients, our clients care about us. There is no greater way to stimulate or encourage loyalty than putting *Clients First*. People remain our clients through thick and thin, and we are their agents no matter what. Just as we want them to succeed, they want us to succeed. Our clients recommend us to others. They sing our praises. They are raving fans. This is the result of deciding that nothing else matters as long as you keep clients by doing what is best for them. A *Clients First* business thrives on word of mouth.

Staying with Us

In the declining market of 2007–2008, most homes did not sell, and the few that sold took longer to sell. The time-on-market average for active listings approached eight months, and the average term for a listing was six months. As a result, agents lost clients to a new listing agent only to turn around and list homes that another agent had just lost. It was like a game of musical chairs, except that it involved houses and agents, and the music conveyed disappointment and despair. Through all this, we lost very few clients. It was humbling to see clients sign listing extension after listing extension with us. In that period, home prices fell by half, and many of our sellers chased the market downward, as we advised reduction after reduction. Again, we were gratified that our clients believed what we told them about the market and worked with us as we all scrambled to deal with an unprecedented situation. Because our clients knew we cared about them, they *stood by us*. Because they stayed with us, we ultimately sold their properties more quickly than neighbors were able to achieve months later—and at higher sales prices.

We lost a few clients during that time. We couldn't blame them. It was a terrifying time. Afterward, the most touching experience of all was that many came back to us. Clients rarely return. This is understandable, because they often leave an agent on bad terms. They are angry, disillusioned, frustrated, or all of these. They have made a decision to move on and have no reason to change their minds. Sometimes, they are simply too embarrassed to return.

We knew nothing of their experiences while they were away from us, but whatever they experienced, it wasn't *Clients First*. They came back. They overcame their prior reasoning. They overcame their embarrassment and they returned to Those Callaways. This is the power of putting *Clients First*.

Once our clients have experienced *Clients First*, they don't want to compromise. We sell a lot of homes where the clients are moving some distance away. They are moving to another city, another part of the country, or even to another country. We get calls. "How do I find an agent here who does things like you do?" We try to help them find the best agent for their areas, but we have never found an agent who approaches real estate sales the way we do. I think many agents are honest, competent, and caring, but we have yet to find a team effort to put *Clients First*. Yet we hope there will be many in the future, and we will gladly recommend them.

Caring is the third key. When combined with key number one, *honesty*, and key number two, *competence*, caring completes the transformation ordained by the commitment to put the client first. Forgo all else as long as you keep the client.

With Great Power

In discovering the three keys and unveiling them here, JoAnn and I have been struck by the immense power given to the holder of these precious gifts. These keys combine to create a great synergy whereby the whole is so much greater than the sum of its parts.

Yes, *Clients First* is a powerful and life-changing concept. With great power comes great responsibility, and *Clients First* is a demanding taskmaster. You cannot pick and choose whom you put first. You must make every client feel as though he or she is number one. *Clients First* demands consistent application. You cannot tinker with *Clients First*. There won't be a *Clients First* 2.0 or a "new" *Clients First* in the future.

Only when you hold all three keys, whole and complete, will you find yourself in rare company.

10 A Rare Thing Indeed

A real estate agent should be ranked as one of our most respected professionals. We take people through what is usually the biggest financial transaction of their lives. We protect them from legal entanglements and unfortunate consequences. We make sure they have done everything they need to do, from buying insurance to turning on the utilities. When they are selling and buying at the same time, we are there to keep everything smooth and on time.

There is no greater responsibility JoAnn and I have felt than when our client is selling a home for the last time. More often than not, most of the person's wealth is represented by the equity in his or her home. Other than monthly retirement checks, this will be the last appreciable sum of money the person will have.

When you are sick, you need a doctor. When you are accused or harmed, you need an attorney. When you buy or sell your home, you need a Realtor. Actually, most people do not realize that while all Realtors are licensed agents, not all agents are Realtors. The Realtor trademark indicates that an agent is a member of the National Association of Realtors. This association holds agents to the highest ethical standards and provides continuing education opportunities to keep members up to date. The state and local associations work hand in hand with the Multiple Listing Services and each state's department of real estate to ensure the public is protected and well served.

The Sad Truth

Why are lawyer jokes so popular? Why do medical malpractice rates skyrocket? Why do so many people think they can just put out a sign and sell their house when they wouldn't think of performing their own appendectomy? The sad truth is that not all clients feel they are being put first. In rare instances, some clients are *put last* and, when that happens, everybody gets to hear about it.

Years ago, one of the women on the television show *The View* became very negative about Realtors. She must have just sold a multi-million-dollar property, because she ragged on her agent and on the industry in general, summing up her remarks with a reference to her Realtor's unconscionable commission, which I'm sure on a luxury property was sizable. The next day, the then-president of the National Association of Realtors publicly demanded an apology. It bounced back and forth in the news, and the whole thing blew over in a day or two, but JoAnn and I remember it. Whenever a client is underserved or an agent is maligned, it saddens our hearts.

I want to believe that the media star's agent who earned that "unconscionable commission" deserved every penny, that he or she works very hard and makes many arduous efforts that terminate in no commission at all, and that the agent takes good care of clients. But this client felt underserved—and this client was on television.

There is an old saying, "Please a hundred people, and one might say something good about you. Fail one person, and that person will surely tell a hundred of your evil." In that saying lies the answer to why there are so many lawyer and doctor and agent jokes. There are a few displeased patients and clients out there.

Raving Fans

Well, where are all the well-served, happy clients? Even if only one in a hundred speaks up, the 6 million to 7 million annual transactions nationwide should yield 60,000 to 70,000 raving fans singing their agents praises. Were this case, the grievous errors of a few would be drowned out by the cheers of the many, and real estate agents would be among our most respected professionals.

Of course, this assumes that, discounting the few troublemakers, all the remaining agents put their *Clients First*. Sadly, this is not the case.

JoAnn and I think very highly of our colleagues. We believe helping people through their biggest purchases, helping them through the uprooting and transitioning from one home to another, is a noble pursuit. We are grateful for the privilege of working in the real estate business. We know many agents share these feelings. Real estate agents are the best of citizens. They typically care about their clients, their neighborhoods, and their communities. They volunteer time and money to worthy causes. They support their local schools. They try to be honest and competent, and they have empathy for their clients' situations. But until they embrace *Clients First*, until they commit to complete honesty, total competence, and unwavering care, they will find their work less rewarding and their satisfaction fleeting.

Many Come Close

Every Christmas, we send out more than 5,000 handmade ornaments to agents with whom we have completed a transaction. Many put their clients first and have become dear friends. Agents compete for clients, but once they have a seller's listing or a buyer in the car, the agent community works together in a spirit of cooperation to bring buyers and sellers together. In negotiations, JoAnn relies on that other agent to be completely forthright, and she expects the other agent to feel the same way about her. It is a small world, and agents who do not honor this code are quickly purged from the fraternity.

Many agents come close to *Clients First*, but it is a rare thing indeed to find a person who holds all three keys, whole and complete.

Before that dark and stormy night, JoAnn and I were good people. We tried to be good parents to our children and good children to our parents. We worked hard and tried to do good jobs. We gave time and money to those who were in need. We supported our government. We voted and went to church, though not enough of either to avoid occasional feelings of guilt. But until we committed to *Clients First* we were not completely honest, totally competent, and unwaveringly caring.

How much of each key we possessed on any given day varied with the situation. We were normal. Then we were changed, and our clients became our advocates, and we gained the respect of our fellow agents and the respect of all those with whom we did business.

You must possess all three keys—*honesty*, *competence*, and *caring*—before you can open the door to the magic room of *Clients First*.

A Single Straw

Do you ever wonder how old sayings came to be? Picture a North African farmer as poor as the dirt he cultivates. One day he collects his camel, the only thing he owns of real value, and begins loading his meager harvest into baskets tied to an old leather harness. Pitchfork by pitchfork, he fills the baskets until all is done. The old camel is not what he used to be and struggles under the load. Just then, the peasant spies a straw in the corner of the loading stall. He bends to retrieve the slip of grass and then tosses it high to land in the uppermost basket. An awful shriek fills the air as the camel feels the crack of one vertebrae and then another. The animal falls to the ground, crying in agony, as the impoverished man helplessly observes the catastrophic event.

So many bad things happen this way. One small thing touches off disaster. Whether it's the straw that broke the camel's back or the theory that the single beat of a butterfly's wings can birth a hurricane halfway around the world, small events can be tipping points that cause very large events to follow.

If this works for bad things, is it possible the same holds true for good things as well? The laws of physics hold that for every action in the universe there is an equal and opposite reaction. Without good, we cannot define evil. If small tipping points set us on the road to ruin, there must be small tipping points that set us on the road to success. In the arts, it's called *getting a key break*. In the corporate world, it can be called *being in the right place at the right time*. Many a politician owes his or her career to just a few votes in a small primary.

The Tipping Point

Many people hold the three keys in various stages of completeness. Without realizing it, they may even hold two keys and need only the tiniest fraction of the third to have it all. But until they hold 100 percent of all three keys, they cannot unlock the door to success. That last tiny fraction of a key is the tipping point.

The difference between an agent who holds *almost* all three keys and the agent who has taken *ownership* of all three keys, whole and complete, is the difference between a lifetime of struggle and a future of ease.

Remember, *Clients First* makes demands, and the first of these is total commitment to the three keys. When you hold these keys, you will feel the power of *Clients First* multiplied through synergy,

The second demand made by *Clients First* is that you treat all clients equally. You must apply *Clients First* universally and you must never, ever give up.

11 Giving Up

There is a school of thought that reasons there are some clients whom you are better off without. Some base this on the Pareto principle, which suggests that 80 percent of your problems come from 20 percent of your clients.

Pareto was an Italian economist who first applied this idea to wealth distribution. He observed that 80 percent of the wealth resided with 20 percent of the population. Since that time, the 80/20 rule has been applied to practically everything, from how you should manage your time to your daily intake of calories.

While this 80/20 rule may or may not apply to problem clients, there are ample alternative theories. A highly successful agent we know follows the teachings of L. Ron Hubbard, the founder of Scientology. Hubbard discovered that a percentage of people are incorrigible and therefore dangerous to those with whom they come into contact. Hubbard estimates that 2.5 percent, or 5 out of every 200 people, are sociopaths with no moral compass and that association with this element can lead to emotional ruin. Hubbard then estimates that 20 percent of the people we know are suppressive personalities. These people, according to Hubbard, are devoted to finding fault with everything and everybody. Association with suppressive personalities is therefore dangerous and to be avoided.

A number of America's corporate gurus propound the theory that you should always be looking to rid the company of the bottom

10 percent. The bottom 10 percent of the employees are not doing the job, are polluting the rest of the workforce, and should therefore be replaced with a new 10 percent, which will be 90 percent contributive and 10 percent lackluster, and so on and so forth. Get rid of the bottom 10 percent of your stores. Close the bottom 10 percent of inefficient factories. Nothing is safe from the corporate reorganizer.

Who's Firing Whom?

Whether following Pareto's 80/20 rule, Hubbard's suppressive personality profile, or any number of other propositions that weed out the troublemakers, the nonperformers, and the unprofitable, professionals often seek to judge a prospective client's potential. The agent wants to eliminate the ones who may be hostile or difficult to satisfy.

When carried a step further, why stop at the unruly? Why not eliminate the potentially low-profit or unprofitable clients? Taken a few steps further, an agent may eliminate all sorts of groups.

In an effort to succeed in this venture of avoiding troublesome clients, professionals find all sorts of ways to qualify the client. They use questionnaires. They figuratively set up hoops for clients to jump through. "Oops, you didn't jump through hoop number three and come in for a pre-home-showing interview, so we won't work with you."

Although professionals serve clients and clients hire professionals, it is not unheard for doctors to say they fired this patient or lawyers to say they fired that client. In fact, many trainers, coaches, and teachers in the real estate business suggest that the road to success and life balance lies in firing bad clients. How did we get to this? A client is not ours to fire. A client is ours to serve; if we cannot or will not do so, it is for the client to fire us.

How does all of this fit with *Client's First*? Do we call it 80 percent of *Clients First*? How about if we say, "Just the profitable *Clients First*"? JoAnn and I have never been able to make those distinctions. *Clients First* means *Clients First*, and if we are asked to serve, we serve.

Emotions

Over the years we have served thousands of clients in a very emotional environment. Residential resale is our chosen specialty, and it is fraught with emotions. People's homes are their havens. For many, their homes define who they are. Jean Auel's classic novel, *The Clan of the Cave Bear*, opens with a family of cave dwellers looking for a new home. The emotion Auel conveys regarding this family's feelings thousands of years ago is no different than today. They are displaced and fearful. They are elated when they find a new cave.

It comes as no surprise that we have dealt with many clients who at one point or another in the process of selling a home and finding a new one simply go crazy. They fall apart early or they fall apart late. Some are wrecks from day one until they've successfully moved, and sometimes their anguish persists. Were we to fire every client who displayed symptoms of distress, we would probably be struggling to operate a used bookstore today and eating macaroni and cheese for dinner.

I sometimes think the entire real estate support industry is made up of good people who tried residential resale first and could not take the emotional toll. Many lenders, commercial agents, model-home salespeople, and title officers have real estate licenses. They will say something like, "Oh, I tried residential sales, but it wasn't for me." Now, these are able people. They are highly successful in their current fields. They just didn't want to be exposed to people's emotional extremes, which inevitably surface when selling or buying houses.

Since we made our commitment to putting *Clients First*, real estate has been the perfect fit for JoAnn and me. Clients tell us of their turmoil, and we don't *feed it back to them*. They unload their burdens and we accept them. Remember, caring is about being the client, and in this instance, caring is about taking on their worries, insecurities, and fears.

It is part of the service, and we do it for hundreds of clients at a time. At any given moment, we might have 150 listings, 40 or 50 properties in escrow, and dozens and dozens of buyers looking for homes. They are all emotional, and they are all our clients, and in 14 years we have yet to fire a single one.

Opportunity to Help

Yes, it would be nice to have a crystal ball. We could gaze into the glass and see our futures. We would make all the right choices. We would have seen the housing bubble of 2005 coming and sold our homes at the high point. We would have purchased the right car when gas went through the roof. We would've, should've, and could've. And yes, we would have picked only the good, loyal, and easy-to-work-with clients.

In the process, however, we would have failed to serve the truly distressed. We would have missed opportunities to help those in need. We would have failed ourselves, and we would not have an army of supporters.

JoAnn and I have found there seems to be another rule, a one-in-a-hundred rule: If you serve a hundred easy clients, one may tell someone of the easy job you did; but if you truly serve one difficult client, that person will tell a hundred people of your struggle to assist him or her in reaching the desired goal.

Never Give Up

We have never bought into the philosophy that advises cherry-picking your clients. We serve every client, and although with some clients the return on our investment of time, energy, emotions, and money may be small or result in a loss, we are rewarded every day with the satisfaction of overcoming obstacles and achieving our clients' goals.

We like to believe there is a karma bank out there somewhere and that when times are particularly difficult or a client is a real stinker, we are making deposits in that bank and that our good karma is earning interest. We have experienced this phenomenon in our business, and whatever you want to call it (reputation, goodwill, branding, or karma), when you put out good things they come back to you multiplied many times over.

Churchill said, as he urged his people to resist Hitler's relentless air attacks on London, "We will never, never, never, never give up." And that is what *Clients First* taught us: We never give up on a client—never.

The search for *Clients First* was arduous, and the discovery of the three keys was exhilarating. To finally be able to define an invisible force that changed our lives was a moment for which we will be forever grateful.

To learn of its synergetic power we feel energized every day.

To be charged with the responsibilities of total commitment to the three keys and the universal application of *Clients First* we are sobered. Knowing that *Clients First* is a timeless principle that will never go out of style, we are reassured.

12 Timeless

Labels are fashionable. We read a book about generation X, or *60 Minutes* devotes a segment of the program to generation Y. We go to a seminar about doing business with millennials, and we take classes to prepare for all those baby boomers who are about to retire. We hear all these labels and think they are new.

More than 2,400 years ago, Socrates complained about the youth of his day. Maybe he called them "generation epsilon." I know the Great Depression of the 1930s left its mark on my parents and grandparents. People who came of age in the 1960s had Vietnam, civil rights, and free love. Everyone grows up at some time or another, and labels make us think that older or younger people are somehow different from us.

What All People Want

In 1600, Shakespeare wrote, "What's in a name? That which we call a rose by any other name would smell as sweet." *Clients First* assertions are similar: A client is a client is a client. Clients come in all sizes, shapes, colors, ages, and dispositions. Clients have varied needs, wants, desires, and dreams. They come across softly. They boom. They demand. They plead, cajole, laugh, and cry. No two clients are the same, and it is in this marvelous variety that JoAnn and I find much enjoyment.

We love getting to know our clients. We chat with couples about how they met. We ask about their careers, hobbies, children, and memorable experiences. With some clients, it is a gradual process; with others, it all comes tumbling out. Yet they all share something of themselves because we are interested in them. We care.

Labels don't matter. They are clients, and we treat them all with respect and honesty. All this talk about social networking is really just a search for the truth. People seek the reassurance of others in that quest for the best answer to any question. Whether they use a computer to access the search engine Google or ask their mothers or rely on handshakes, people want the truth.

I don't care whom the client is, that person will resent slipshod service, whether it is from a clerk who misses the customer's hand and drops coins on the floor for lack of attention to the client or from a doctor who removes the wrong kidney. Clients want competence. Old folks want competence. Newlyweds want competence. Everyone appreciates a job well done and despises being mistreated when the work is poor.

Clients First is timeless. The three keys are timeless. Labels are fashion, and fashion changes like the leaves on the trees. But _Clients First_ never lets you down. _Clients First_ is a little black dress or a well-tailored blue suit. _Clients First_ works with all clients.

The Rich

When F. Scott Fitzgerald penned the words, "The rich are different from you and me," he implied that money created a divide between people. Hemingway referred to the haves and have-nots.

I remember the first transaction we handled for over $1 million. I was so nervous I had to rewrite the contract twice, and I had previously never had to rewrite a contract even once. JoAnn later asked if I was okay. She was concerned that I was coming down with something.

When I told her that I was fine, she took my hand and said, "These are just clients, and we will take care of them just like all the others." JoAnn knew. She knew that while my upbringing was middle class, I came from a working-class family tree. The rich were different, and I was on the other side of that great divide.

Today, thanks to *Clients First* and an incredible amount of good fortune, JoAnn and I are financially secure. We are modestly rich, yet we are no different. A dear friend once quoted an old Jewish proverb, "Once poor, never rich." We still feel the same as always. JoAnn puts change in Mason jars as if we might need those pennies, nickels, dimes, and quarters to buy food someday. Every time I use a paper towel, I feel rich, because my mother cut up old clothes to use as cleaning rags.

The rich don't like being lied to any more or any less than hourly workers who are told that their timecard shows they are late—when they know the boss sets the clock ahead. The rich don't appreciate lousy service any more or any less than hot dog vendors do when the bun order comes in with all sesame seeds. And the rich don't care any more or any less about themselves than the GI just trying to get home from Afghanistan. When it comes to the three keys and *Clients First*, the rich are no different from you and me, and when they are clients, you simply put them first along with all the rest.

The Guilty

Would JoAnn and I be better off without the tough clients? Maybe. Would we be less stressed? I don't know.

We recently heard a gentleman speak to a group of real estate agents who represented banks in selling their foreclosure properties. He pointed out the government wanted homeowners to first attempt to modify their mortgage terms—and only if that effort failed should the home go to short sale or foreclosure. This was not a popular notion with this group, as their livelihood depended on a flow of bank-owned houses to sell. The speaker pointed out that of the loans that were modified, more than 90 percent would end up back in default and go into foreclosure anyway. All the agents nodded their heads, agreeing that this was a terrible waste of time and effort. This modification process could delay the sales process by a year or more. These homes were tied up by wasted effort. The government, they all agreed, should just let the homes go back to the banks so that these agents could sell them.

Then the speaker referred to our system of justice, which presumes innocence. He quoted the old adage that it is better for ten guilty individuals to go free than for one innocent person to be punished. The next thing he said moved this somewhat jaded, yet not insensitive, crowd, for they had all seen, firsthand, children's toys left in an empty house or a family dog unfed and abandoned in an overgrown yard. He said, "If we are able to save only a few home-owners from the anguish of losing their homes, then the loan modification program is worth it." The crowd cheered. Without regard to their personal lucre, they applauded, because it was true and, we all felt better for hearing this man say it. You have to do the right thing, and serving every client is the right thing to do.

The Evil People

Is it easy to do the right thing? Not always. The long-suffering would argue that it is never easy—always hard. I think *Clients First* makes it easier, because by putting the *Client First* you are already on the doing-the-right-thing path. JoAnn and I have had some awful clients. To ease the tension, we called them "the evil people," for they were deeply hurtful. Out of more than 5,000 clients, we could probably number them on the fingers of two hands, but they were memorable. Was there a way to avoid these evil people? I think not. They came from nowhere in the middle of otherwise normal transactions. We could not have weeded them out with a questionnaire nor seen it in their eyes nor predicted their behavior based on the way they dressed. Had we tried, we would have lost many wonderful clients in the effort.

We did the best we could with these undesirable clients and moved on. In retrospect, there were lessons to be learned from these experiences. I might have preferred to learn these insights from a book or a lecture or heard about them from another agent, but they were nonetheless valuable teachings.

Lifted Up

I look back on these clients as the price of admission to a grand show. *Clients First* is a thrilling performance to be enjoyed with an open heart. Our clients have enriched us far more than a few pieces of silver would. They have boosted our self-worth. They have brought us joy and prosperity of spirit. They have made each day something to look forward to, because in putting them first, in caring about their needs and aspirations, we were lifted up.

Clients First is timeless. It does not go in and out of style. It does not prejudge or discriminate. And it makes everything easy.

These are the demands and responsibilities of *Clients First*. Commit totally to the three keys; apply *Clients First* universally; and know that it is timeless and requires no changes. Fulfill these and you will be amazed at the power of *Clients First*, because this concept is greater than the sum of its parts. *Clients First* has synergy.

13 Synergy of the Three Keys

JoAnn often says, "I would never do this business without Joseph." Then, like an "I love you, too," I agree and say the same thing to her. But it's more than an "I love you, too." While I think JoAnn could, I don't believe I have all the tools. What we do have is synergy.

As related in the introduction Marge read at the Mustang Library, JoAnn is good with people and I am good with paper. Of course, this is an oversimplification meant for effect with an audience. The truth is that JoAnn is perfectly capable of handling any contract, form, or memorandum, and I speak with dozens of people a day. But our respective strengths are, for JoAnn, being able to understand a client's situation and, for me, going to the heart of any document. This makes us a great team. Sometimes we joke that between us we have the makings of one pretty good agent.

Actually, between the two of us we have something far more than one good agent. We have something that confounds mathematicians and puzzles logicians. What we have is one plus one makes three. Sometimes the combination equals four or five . . . or even infinity. When you combine two things, and the total is far greater than the sum of the two parts, you have *synergy*.

Have you ever felt this strange effect in your life? How much more difficult is it to parent as (or to be parented by) a single mother or a single father than when two share the load? Could Lewis have reached the Pacific Ocean without Clark? Could Leiber have changed popular music without Stoller? Have you ever watched on a given Sunday when a team that shouldn't win comes together and knocks off an undefeated foe? This is synergy, and it is something available for anyone to harness.

Our World Changed

When JoAnn and I combined honesty with competence with caring, we unleashed a powerful synergy that changed our lives and suddenly made everything easy.

Our lives before *Clients First* had been a series of ups and downs, anticipations and disappointments, successes and failures. We were like most folks. Life was often a struggle. Suddenly, our lives became a progression of ups and ups, expectations exceeded, and undreamed of successes. It was as if a logjam had broken and now everything was flowing in the same direction.

I know of no other way to explain what was happening than by using the word *synergy*. At the time, these three key changes seemed small. As we were going through the process of first deciding to undo that one transaction and then passing our decision on to Marta and Susan, we were excited at the way we felt without knowing why. We felt good. But we had no idea that this was some monumental moment in our lives.

I'm sure our forefathers were sober men as they penned the Declaration of Independence and later the US Constitution, but I doubt they had any idea about the vast consequences of their actions. You simply don't think about making history. John Adams was probably preoccupied with his family's needs, and Benjamin Franklin may have been more concerned with a new ache or pain that morning. They had no idea what was to come and how they would change the world. I have no delusions that *Clients First* is as important as a government of the people, by the people, and for the people, but it nonetheless has a synergetic power to change lives.

Clients First changed our world. We were free. We no longer had to think about what we were saying or what we had said. Whatever we said was the truth, or else we didn't say it. The only challenge was to *know* the truth, and it's surprising how easy that becomes when your goal is honesty. Whatever we said was competent, or else we didn't say it. How liberating it is to acknowledge your limitations and say, "I'll find out." Whatever we said was anchored in a deep and passionate desire to get what our client wanted. The synergy that results from the combination of the three keys gave us the gift of freedom.

Satisfaction

Our relationships with our clients became enjoyable. We work all the time, yet it never seems like work. Our work is one long series of enjoyable exchanges with people we help. Because we are honest, competent, and caring, we help people a lot. And the ones we've helped the most are the ones we remember the best. A reporter once asked us to name the dollar amount of our largest sale. I couldn't recall without taking a long pause to think about it. The clients we've helped the most, however, jump to the forefront. There was the time we moved Mr. Williams to a small condo. This was to be his last move, and all he had was the equity in his house. We got him top dollar and made sure he bought in a safe neighborhood while conserving his cash. He had been a clockmaker, and we helped him sell all his clocks. We supervised the movers and made sure his refrigerator was stocked. I have no idea how much commission we earned, but we will never forget how good we felt.

A Jillion Megawatts

The greatest power of this synergy is how *Clients First* changes the clients themselves. Without getting all mystical here, clients have a way of knowing when you are lying to them, when you don't know what you are doing, or when you don't really care. Clients feel what is being broadcast on that invisible wavelength we call *intuition*. They know, and with the synergy of *Clients First* in the atmosphere, it's as if the volume has been pumped up to 100 decibels. It's like the broadcast station is on steroids and putting out a jillion megawatts. It is the synergy of the three keys at work, and one plus one plus one is equal to infinity.

This synergy is a beacon that lights the way for people to find you. Clients come and bring their friends. It's shameful to say, but this combination of honesty, competence, and caring is not often found. I had a screenwriting teacher once tell me that a good movie script would be found even if it were locked in the trunk of a car traveling the freeways at three o'clock in the morning. He said that there were so many bad scripts in Hollywood that one good script would glow neon, and a film producer would find himself out there in his car and would be compelled to stop that strange vehicle in the wee hours and not have any idea why. That's how it works. People are compelled, and they do not know why. We thank clients for their referrals every day, but we have yet to ask for one. Thank goodness we have the power of *Clients First* to bring them in the door.

Queens to Swoon

This is synergy: the combination of ingredients that result in something much larger than its recipe. Synergy takes over when you combine honesty, competence, and caring. You end up with something that can change your world. But what happens if you measure out the ingredients and cut a few corners? What happens if you don't mix in a full measure of honesty, 100 percent of competence, and all the care you can muster? Will you end up baking an ordinary cake with all the synergy of the plastic platter it sits on? Or will you bake a cake that drives kings to ecstasy and causes queens to swoon? This is the power of *Clients First*, and this is the power of synergy.

Is it really that simple? Could three keys really have such extraordinary power? Aren't other qualities and activities necessary to put *Clients First*? One might think so. JoAnn and I certainly made copious lists. Remember how we discussed and debated for hours on end? We watched what happened each day in our own business. I originally came up with a list of 122 ways to put *Clients First* and could have added to it until I reached 1,000. We narrowed it down to less than a dozen, but when we applied the requirement that they be essential, that without this key, you could not put a *Client First*, we were left with only three. Not that the others on the list weren't important, even vital, but they were either a part of one of the three keys or they were simply not essential. We called them "first runners-up."

14 And the First Runner-Up Is . . .

It is widely accepted yet often forgotten that the difference between winning and losing, between first place and second place, between stardom and toil is most often small. Sometimes the difference is infinitely small. Water freezes at 32 degrees. At 33 degrees, it is simply water. At 212 degrees it boils. Again, at 211 degrees, it is water. One degree makes the difference.

From a fourteenth-century proverb, we are reminded, "For want of a nail . . . a kingdom was lost." In sports, we watch as the winners of Olympic gold medals are decided in thousandths of a second. Baseball addicts are quick to point out that the difference between being a major-league player and languishing in obscurity is just one extra base hit out of every 20 times at bat. Many young people memorize the presidents of the United States, but how many can recite the campaign losers?

Just before they crown Miss Universe, they announce the first runner-up, a beautiful woman who most probably lost by a half point on a single judge's scorecard. Yet she goes home to her country and takes her sash to the drycleaners for ultimate placement in an heirloom box.

As JoAnn and I searched for the keys to *Clients First*, we didn't know whether there would be three keys, five rules, or seven commandments; we were searching for the concepts that were *essential*. As we tested virtues and attributes, methods and systems, we asked the question, "Is this essential to making clients first?" You cannot say you put your clients first if you lie to them, offer incompetent products or services, or don't care about what they want. All three keys are required, and all three require 100 percent effort. You cannot skimp on one of the keys or cut a corner here or there. Your commitment to *Clients First* must be complete.

That said, the world is full of *Clients First* runners-up, and many are almost as important as the three keys. The difference is that none of these are essential all the time. These virtues do, however, deserve mention here.

Gratitude

JoAnn and I are so grateful. We are grateful for that night when we found *Clients First*, or maybe it's the other way around: Maybe *Clients First* found us. Either way, we are thankful every day, especially the fourth Thursday in November. We thank our clients early and we thank our clients often. Letting them know we appreciate their business makes them feel good. It shows them we care.

Before Kmart closed, I told people to remember TYFSAK. When they asked what in the world I was talking about (and they often did), I told them to go shopping at Kmart and, when checking out, to lean around to view the little sign facing the cashier. It says TYFSAK, which stands for "Thank You For Shopping At Kmart." I hope Kmart gave credit to the creative person who came up with that little sign, because if you ever shopped at Kmart, I assure you, you heard the cashier say thank you.

On Christmas morning, a transformed Ebenezer Scrooge was thankful it wasn't too late, and he went to Bob Cratchit's home to express his gratitude for Cratchit's years of service. Perhaps you know someone like Scrooge, who cannot express his or her gratitude. Maybe it is you. Make gratitude a part of your day. Is there someone you need to thank? Do it now. Do it often.

Many times, JoAnn and I have experienced low times. Life is not only about business and, in spite of our recent success, life is not just a bowl of cherries. The best tool we have to cope with those moments is to count our blessings. No matter how bad things may seem, when we start to count the things we can be thankful for, things begin to get better. Sometimes the first thing on the list is that it could be worse. Of course, then we have to knock on wood, and if we are in the car that can be a whole new problem. But the point is that gratitude is a powerful emotion. It can heal. It can build. And in the case of putting *Clients First*, gratitude can be an ally.

Respect

When JoAnn and I heard Jack Nicholson's character in the movie *A Few Good Men* shout from the witness stand, "You can't handle the truth!" we were shocked. Although this man believed himself to be our protector, he had no respect for the American people. Our shock was at this officer's disrespect for those he served.

I had always thought respect was about being polite and courteous with people. Yes ma'am, no sir—we were always respectful. But I came to realize when putting clients first that respect is about letting people make their own decisions. The clients' decisions are sacrosanct, and whenever you take that away from people you're acting disrespectful. How can you allow your clients to base their decisions on less than a full understanding of the facts and the freedom to deliberate? Honesty shows respect.

Can you do a poor job for someone and then say at the end of the day that you respect your client (i.e., your employer)? No. When you work for others, you should respect their money as if it were yours. You should respect their time as if it were yours. You should respect their situations as if they were yours. You should do these things because, when you care, you become the client.

How many times do we see people treated differently because of the way their circumstances are perceived? People who are thought to be financially successful are treated better than those who are thought to be impoverished. We are all shocked when the big shot turns out to be a crook and the ragged old woman turns out to have a mattress full of cash. We should have known about him. We should have been nicer to her. Actually, we should have given everyone all the respect we could.

When you are *honest* with clients, you are respecting their ability and right to make up their own minds based on the truth. When you are *competent* with clients, you are respecting their right to receive full value for their money. When you *care* about clients, you are respecting their hopes, dreams, desires, and, yes, misgivings, insecurities, and flaws. Your commitment to *Clients First* demands that you respect them, and the three keys make it a reality.

Communication

Silence is a punishment. Years ago, we had a neighbor whose husband would not speak to her for weeks at a time. It was one of the cruelest things I ever witnessed. We moved away, and I don't know what happened to them but I'll never forget the pain that emanated from that poor woman.

You must communicate with your customers. The simple acts of naming your business, creating a logo, and branding your product are basic communication tasks, but you cannot stop there. You must relate to clients what you can do for them. You must tell people how you are going to do it and, ultimately, that you delivered.

My mother got my first job for me. I was 13, bright and shy. The local druggist put me behind the soda counter and showed me how to make malts and sundaes. Then he left, and I had to relate to the customers. I was fine with the first one. The woman knew what she wanted, and I prepared and served it without a word. Then I got three customers at once and I had to decide whom to serve first. I needed to speak and keep everyone happy. A simple "you're next" would have worked wonders, but I couldn't talk. As their impatience grew, I became rattled. I didn't even know how to ask for the money. I was a math whiz in school. Making change would be easy, but I couldn't even announce the completion of my task and tell the poor customer the price. At the end of three hours, I went home in tears. I never returned.

Can you put *Clients First* without communicating with them? I suppose if you were a deaf-mute mule train operator in Venezuela, you could be successful, but you would still have to have someone to negotiate rates and delivery. You can't be honest without telling the truth. You can't be competent without clear instructions and agreed-upon goals. You can't express care without an exchange of thoughts and feelings. Communication is the medium, and the three keys are the message.

One of the reasons our clients feel we put them first is that we tell them just that. We tell them that all we care about is what is best for them. We express this, along with our gratitude, often.

Things don't always go smoothly. In fact, some days are just one long bumpy road. Houses don't sell, deals fall apart, people's situations change. JoAnn and I often have to remind ourselves that we don't earn our keep by serving the easy ones. Rather, it's the difficult ones who justify our efforts. Sometimes, clients call ready for a fight. Things aren't going well and they are frustrated. Often, no matter what the real reason, they blame their agents. After all, we were supposed to take care of them. I have found the best response is never disagreement; it is never a rational review of the facts; it is never a review of the reason for their frustration; it is the simple communication that all that matters is what is best for them. That phrase has fixed so many situations, and in the others it was a start toward a solution. This is how you put *Clients First*. You tell them.

Obedience

Dogs are loyal, and they love unconditionally, but the difference between a good dog and a bad dog is obedience. Soldiers follow orders. Cooks prepare your meal the way you want it. When it's *your* money, you want to receive what you pay for. If you are paying for a service, then the provider should deliver what you ask for. To serve is to be obedient.

Does this mean the clients always know what is best? No, but it is not our place to save them. They must save themselves. It is our place to serve them. By being honest, competent, and caring we help them make their decisions, and we hope these are better decisions because of our care. But, in the end, we give them what they want and do what they say. This is putting the *Client First*.

All of these virtues add to the *Clients First* experience. Be kind, courteous, generous, friendly, and sincere. To do less is to regret the time lost in pointless endeavors.

Be an advocate. Promise less and deliver more. Be as determined for your clients as you would be for yourself.

Put your *Clients First*, and do not limit your efforts on their behalf. Be honest, competent, and caring. Then build on this foundation. Remember, the difference between a champion and an also-ran is often immeasurably small.

Clients First Makes All the Difference

15

"Show Me," Said the Missourian

In grade school we learn arithmetic and to check our work. You check your addition of three plus five equals eight by then subtracting either five from eight to get three or three from eight to get five. Sounds simple enough, unless you are a six-year-old, in which case the concept takes several months to master. From there you move on to multiplication, which you check by dividing, and division, which you check by multiplying. Then they change the name from *arithmetic* to *mathematics*, and it gets really complicated, but the point is that you need to check your work. You find a way to prove your answer.

At last, JoAnn and I had our answer to the question posed by the lady in blue at the Mustang Library: "But what is the *real* reason for your success?" At last, we knew that the answer was a two word miracle: *Clients First*. Finally, we could say that the secret to unlocking the door to immense success was to hold the three keys of *honesty*, *competence*, and *care*. And we knew the great power of this concept and the great responsibility that comes with it.

Skeptics Might Say . . .

But how do we prove it? It is simply not enough to stand on the street corner, stomp our feet, and insist it is true because we just know it to be so. Skeptics might say, "Oh, you two are just brilliant businesspeople and you would have succeeded anyway." Then why *hadn't* we? Remember, we were both past 50 when we stumbled into the real estate business. Where was all this brilliance before? Not that JoAnn and I are stupid, but whatever brilliance we possessed before real estate did not lead to stellar success. Before that dark and stormy night, we were different; we hadn't yet made the commitment to put our *Clients First*, no matter what, and until we made that life-changing decision, whatever brilliance we had was tarnished and unrealized.

Others might credit luck or being in the right place at the right time. We started in the summer of 1997. Mortgage interest rates were 8 to 9 percent. The Phoenix/Scottsdale market had been flat for more than 16 years, ever since the bubble and bust of 1979–1980, followed by the Savings and Loan scandal and the Resolution Trust Corporation bailout. There were a lot more sellers than buyers, and our broker even questioned our choice to start in our quiet ZIP code, which included homes that were more than 20 years old, when all the action (what there was of it) was 5 to 10 miles north of us, where some builders were still developing new subdivisions. Back then, there were more agents leaving the real estate business than there were entering the profession.

What about the bubble of 2005–2006? Didn't every agent get rich then? Many did, but then, almost to the last man, woman, and child, they gave it all back and more. The fact is that if we had not had a bubble and the consequent bust starting in 2007, we would all be better off. Prices of homes in 2011 were back to what they were in the late 1990s when we started out. Besides, we had already achieved our success before the bubble. That we prospered during the bubble was only a further credit to our *Clients First* mission. That we survived the bust is probably the greater victory, and we credit it to the loyal following of our clients through what has been called the worst economic downturn since the Great Depression.

Probably most people in the industry—other agents, title officers, and mortgage lenders—would say that our marketing and our advertising is the real secret to our success. Yes, to be sure, we get a lot of compliments on the ads we run and the postcards we mail. People like our website, although it went live in 2003 and is a dinosaur in technology time. The plain fact is that many other agents market and advertise. Many spend most or all of their money on these activities, yet these efforts only get the clients to come to you. It is what you do with and for the client that makes all the difference. Were it not for *Clients First*, we would have to spend much more, be ever more creative, and, at the end of the day, we would very probably have less business and only the prospect of doing the same things next week, next month, and next year to warm our hearts each night as we contemplated the next day's struggle.

What Is the Formula?

Yes, we have been lucky and we have worked hard. We have invested in marketing, because we know that even executives at McDonald's and Walmart cannot sit on their laurels, no matter how many satisfied followers they have. The reality of the real estate market is that it is cyclical, and there is no right or wrong time to enter it, as opportunities and dangers are always present. The real secret (and, if we are talking secret here, it cannot be what everybody else guesses) is how we treat our clients.

But how do you prove it? How do you know that *Clients First* is the real reason for our success? What is the formula? How do you subtract or divide *Clients First*? Maybe it's not as simple as arithmetic, but the question still cries out. How do we prove our answer, our formula for success?

The scientific community grapples with this question all the time. Scholars have all sorts of rules and procedures by which they move from postulating to theory to scientific laws. Criminal investigators have well-documented methods by which they narrow the field of suspects until they have enough evidence to make an arrest. In our civil courts, cases are decided after a preponderance of evidence has been presented. The medical community argues over the anecdotal proof of naturopaths versus the results of clinical trials. There are probably hundreds of ways to prove or disprove anything. So, how do we prove the validity of *Clients First*?

Our Experience

JoAnn and I struggled with this conundrum almost as much as we did with the original question posed by the lady in blue. We knew we were right. We knew it the moment we narrowed down the list while having Sunday brunch at the Princess. We knew the three keys were the essential pieces that would unlock the door to success. And we knew from our experience with Marta and all the team members and all the clients who followed that this was a truth that could be passed on. This was not only *our* secret, it was a secret we could share. Our proof was our experience with *Clients First*. Our proof lay in the history of our rise in our industry and our market. For this proof, we would have to mine our years of putting the *Client First*, no matter the consequences. Some of our proof is anecdotal. Some of it is based on common sense. Some of it is simple subtraction, by asking what the result would have been had we *not* put the *Client First*. You might say the proof is in the pudding. In the end, our proof is a preponderance of evidence, and you get to be the judge and jury.

Our hope is that you will be a good judge and fair arbiter of the truth. Don't hesitate to be skeptical. If you are from the "Show Me" state of Missouri, then ask, "What if?" Question everything we share, because only in your own personal examination of the evidence will you come to a conclusion that makes you feel confident.

Our hope also is that you will come to accept *Clients First* for what it is and for what it can do for you. We wish you immense success and a changed life, a life fuller and richer for accepting the three keys as your path to putting *Clients First*.

16 Team First

Whether it is Tom Hanks, cast away on an island, or Charlton Heston at the end of *Planet of the Apes*, there is a futility in being alone. Life unshared has no point.

Like you, JoAnn and I have only 24 hours in a day. We can serve only so many clients face-to-face. To expand our business, to leverage ourselves, we need a team.

The ideal team would be a number of clones. JoAnn could manage the JoAnn clones and I could manage the Joseph clones, and we could serve countless more clients. The trouble with cloning is (1) scientists have yet to clone human beings, and (2) when they do there will be a dumb-down effect, with each clone not quite as good as the original. Ego aside, I don't believe the world is ready for a series of ever less intelligent Josephs.

We Leveraged Ourselves

Actually, our first assistant, Marta, was in her own way better than a JoAnn clone or a Joseph clone. She brought her own history and culture and personality to client interactions. She was different from JoAnn and me, and that difference enriched our clients.

Clients First transformed Marta as it had transformed us. *Clients First* was cloned in that moment when Marta said of a dismantled deal, "I'm glad. It really wasn't the best thing for either of them." She was talking, of course, about the Browns and the Smiths with whom we had met the night before. Marta knew that undoing their deal was the right thing to do, and she lived the *Clients First* maxim from that moment on. We leveraged ourselves through Marta, and that was the start of our *Clients First* team.

You might think that Marta's acceptance was a no-brainer. After all, she was right there in our home office. We could hear her interact with clients. We could step in if things went screwy, or Marta could hand off the call if the client preferred talking to JoAnn. Why shouldn't Marta follow our lead?

Vow of Poverty

Let's take a look at someone who was not in our home office, someone we spoke to only a few times a day. JoAnn and Donna hadn't seen each other for a couple of years, but they went way back. Donna was a family friend and had always been a career woman. One day she walked into our open house on Eugie Terrace. At that time, she owned a small patio home with a one-car garage, which was fine until her marriage to Lonnie. They wanted more space, a yard, and a garage for both cars.

We started showing Donna and Lonnie houses, and after about 20 houses we found their honeymoon home. We put the patio home on the market and sold that as well. In the process, Donna expressed a desire to work with us. JoAnn was excited at the idea; she knew what a sincere person Donna was, but the responsibility scared both of us. Donna had a very good position with a technology company that was developing laptop computer screens.

We discussed it over and over for about a week. Donna was making good money. What if real estate wasn't her thing? What if she failed to make a living? JoAnn practically made Donna take a vow of poverty before she let her enroll in real estate school and quit her job. Once we made the commitment, we had to decide how we were going to best utilize Donna's skills.

Sellers Are Not Sitting Next to You in Your Car

Our biggest challenge was *time*—too many clients and too little time. We looked at our business and realized that buyers take a lot more time than sellers. With a seller, you go out and list the property, then spend your time marketing it. The thing is that if you are marketing one house versus 20 houses, you don't spend 20 times as much time on marketing. The sellers are not sitting next to you in your car. With buyers, however, you spend whatever time it takes; if you have 20 buyers, it takes more hours than there are in a day.

We decided that Donna would do all the legwork with the clients, and then, when they were ready to write an offer, we would meet up at a local coffee shop and JoAnn and I would do the paperwork. It sounded simple, but JoAnn and I were emotional wrecks. How could we handle the handoff? What should we say? Our clients were precious to us. We put them first. We cared. How would we know whether Donna was putting our *Clients First*?

We knew that Donna was honest, and we knew that she cared. What we didn't know was whether she could get up to speed on the homes available, whether they were priced right, and how to present them to a prospective buyer. We worked closely with her at first and found out that one of her talents was an uncanny memory for houses. I remember showing 10 houses and getting confused. Donna remembered every house and every detail. It amazes me today that when the subject comes up of a house that was last on the market 10 years ago, Donna will say something like, "Oh yeah, the one with the blue countertops and the Mulberry tree in the backyard with all the leaves falling in the pool."

One Phase of the Process

We weren't asking Donna to know everything there was to know about real estate, although she certainly had to take her classes and pass the state licensing test. We were asking her to serve our clients in one phase of the process: to find the right house for them. Because this was all she did, she became extraordinarily competent for each client who was at that stage in the home buying experience.

Every day, Donna spent hours at the computer searching for homes for sale, and when she went out with a client to show a house, she knew what the client wanted to know: *How long has this been on the market? How much is it? How does it compare to the one down the street?* Since Donna was in and out of probably 200 homes a week, she was an expert when our client needed an expert. This was putting our *Clients First* in high gear, but how would we make the transition?

It did not go smoothly, but then again it did not go badly, either. Each handoff was a new adventure. We stammered, we fumbled, and we took clients back, because Donna couldn't be in two places at once. Over a 12-month period, the process got smoother. Donna did a great job and was well liked by clients.

Through this process, Donna picked up on our example. She saw us putting the clients first, and she heard Marta say it, and it just happened. Today Donna is competent, honest, and caring. She spends all her time showing houses, and our clients are fortunate to work with her.

You Don't Want Me

I had a client call the other day and he wanted to know whether I would be the one showing him houses. I said, "Oh, you don't want me," and gave him to Donna. Were I to show him houses, I would be capable, but I wouldn't be up to the minute on every house out there. Donna knows about every house on the market and remembers them all. She knows which ones are special, which ones are run-down, and which ones are priced right. We put our clients first by introducing them to Donna.

Does Donna want to write a contract? Absolutely not! Donna knows how to complete the paperwork, but she wants the client best served. She puts Clients *First* by handing them off to one of our contract agents. Under JoAnn's supervision, Alicia or Kelly or Joe prepares the contract, calls the listing agent for info, pulls up the property's listing history and comparable sales, and takes the buyer through the offer. JoAnn negotiates the deal, and when we have a seller acceptance, the client's file goes to escrow, where another agent on our team takes him or her from contract to close. *Clients First* created this system, which we call Super Service. And what about the handoff anguish? It doesn't exist. Our clients love working with specialists. They will even ask, "Okay, who do I see next?"

We didn't clone ourselves; we cloned *Clients First.*

A Client of Those Callaways

Today, our team is 30 agents strong, and they all have a two word mission statement: *"Clients First."* They all deal directly with clients, and we never have to look over anyone's shoulder. There is no backbiting or negative competition. A client is never referred to as "Brian's client" or "Joyce's client." Every client is referred to as a client of Those Callaways.

JoAnn and I could never do what we do without this team, and we owe them our deepest gratitude. At the same time, they put their trust and faith in us to keep up the steady flow of buyers and sellers, and, just as they serve our clients, we have a responsibility to our team. It is our role to serve them.

A *team*, by definition, is a group working toward a common cause. In our case, that cause is serving the clients of Those Callaways. Our team is an interdependent group. Each agent at Those Callaways relies on several other team members in order to best serve our clients.

Some teams are like a chain, which is only as strong as its weakest link. Each member of the team provides a specific step in a process. Each team member is dependent upon the team member completing the task that came just prior to the current step. When there is a breakdown at any step in the process, it can be like an assembly line coming to a stop. Everything waits until that link in the chain is fixed and the process is set back in motion.

Some teams are segregated by purpose, such as football teams. You have the offense, the defense, the kickoff team, the field goal team, and the punt return team. There can be further segregation, whereby the offense is divided into the passing team and the running team; in an onside kick situation, the return team switches to the hands team, with all the receivers on the front line. The football team has a common goal, and interdependence between offense and defense is really about getting the ball back.

At Those Callaways, our team is more like a honeycomb than a chain. Every member of the team serves several other members of the team, and they are cross-trained so that if someone is sick or goes on vacation, the other team members take up the slack without delay. Because every client is simply a client of Those Callaways, and because our mission statement is only two words (i.e., *Clients First*), our team is focused on one goal.

An Integral Part of Everyone's Day

Let's take Stuart, for example. Stuart came to work with us shortly after Donna. At that time, whenever we got a listing, Marta would order a post to be installed and I would go out and hang the sign and install the lockbox. It may not sound like much, but it took maybe an hour out of my day that could have been spent working with a buyer or marketing a seller's home. It was important work. Our sellers certainly wanted the sign hung right and the lockbox placed in the best spot. Sometimes, a potential buyer would stop and ask about the new listing as I was doing the work. We asked Stuart to be our property presentation agent and to install the lockboxes.

Stuart could have just done what was asked, and that would have been the end of it. We probably could have just as easily hired a high school student part-time. But Stuart bought into *Clients First* immediately. Stuart didn't see his role as menial, he saw himself as an agent putting *Clients First* and as a team member putting each teammate first.

Today, Stuart is an integral part of everyone's day. Kelly needs someone to attend a potentially difficult home inspection, so she asks Stuart. When there's an important final walk-through, Stuart goes. If a newly listed house needs repairs, Stuart is JoAnn's trusted eyes and ears. If Alicia needs a counteroffer signed and the client doesn't have a fax, Stuart is her man.

Stuart serves every agent in our office. He has saved countless deals because the clients love him. Stuart mentions the clients' needs every day. He is honest, caring, and competent. He has taught us all about *Clients First*. He's not just a problem solver, he's the important problem solver, and, yes, he still hangs signs and installs lockboxes.

They Put Each Other First

Our team is a team of Stuarts. Every agent of Those Callaways serves every other agent. Every agent puts teammates first. *Clients First* gave rise to this team. By simply saying that their mission is to put the *Clients First*, they have, by extension, put each other first.

JoAnn and I lead by example. We treat every member of the team with open honesty. There are no secrets. We owe our team competency. We constantly work to improve our skills at bringing in the business. We strive to lead our team through the good times and bad. We care deeply about each team member. We celebrate holidays and birthdays. We have an Agent of the Year award we present to that team member who best personifies *Clients First*. We have contests and Super Bowl pools. Every Monday and Friday, we have lunch delivered to our office for the agents. At Those Callaways, we put our team first, and our team puts our *Clients First*.

Our clients know this. You can't walk into our offices without knowing this. Our clients love us because we love them. They know we put them first, and it is to them we owe our success.

17 In Their Own Words

To make things fun at our 2006 company Thanksgiving dinner, we announced a Christmas contest for the team. Each entrant was to name three companies that, in their personal experience, put them first and three companies that put them last. They were to explain why and would be judged on clarity, creativity, sincerity, and quality. The prize was to be a one-week trip, including airfare and lodging, to any destination in the world.

Marti

As wonderful as Marti is, she did not win this contest. Marti is the voice of Those Callaways. She answers our phone. Although many companies are satisfied to have an hourly receptionist, we have Marti. She is a licensed real estate agent and has been for more than 30 years; Marti is the first person our clients hear. She brings honesty, competence, and caring to their initial contacts with us. Marti listens. Although she often handles more than 100 calls a day, she listens. She makes every caller her friend. She knows every seller, because she is the one who calls to set up the showing appointments. She knows every agent, because she's the one they rely on to get in to our clients' homes. Marti helps every agent on our Those Callaways team, and many times she has saved a deal. Marti was our Agent of the Year in 2009.

For the contest, Marti went the extra mile and submitted 13 *Clients First* experiences and eight *clients last* debacles. Here are some of the experiences she recounted:

> STARBUCKS. My fiancé, Wade, was one of their best customers while he was alive. Many, many times they would give him free refills, throw in a sweet roll, or give him a gift at Christmas. After he died, I went in to tell them. Everyone stopped what they were doing and came over to me, hugged me, and offered to help in any way they could. Even though my heart was breaking, they were warm and consoling.
>
> DILLARD'S. While looking for a special item, a few sales-people kept on with their duties; then one saleswoman finally helped me. She went with me from department to department helping me find exactly what I wanted. How amazing—and what a difference between salespeople (they are on commission!).
>
> WELLS FARGO BANK. Since I make many deposits, the tellers at the Fry's branch (64th Street and Greenway) know me well. One young man who helps me often knows that I am collecting state quarters for my little grandson. The teller was *SO* customer-oriented that he went through his entire drawer and had four new ones for me that I didn't yet have. That made an impression on me.

You can see Marti is a caring person, because she appreciates caring people, but her examples seemed to rely on each company's luck of the draw in hiring the right people rather than something the company did. Here is one that really angered Marti.

> DOLLAR TREE. A woman standing in the checkout line had been waiting a long time and was next in line to be checked out; her basket was *FULL* of items to be purchased. The person in front of her had a coupon, and the checker didn't know how to handle it, so he called the manager over. The woman in line was very patient and polite. The manager had difficulty as well, and it was taking a *LONG* time. The woman in line made a half-joking comment that if they're going to offer the coupons, they

should know how to check them out. To everyone's surprise and horror, including my own (I, too, was in line waiting), the manager started yelling at the poor woman that he *DID* know how to do it, that *HE* was the *MANAGER* and did *NOT* need to be insulted, and so on. Needless to say, the woman left the store without making a purchase (and it would have been a *BIG* sale).

I guess Dollar Tree was not having a lot of luck in hiring customer-focused managers.

This was a tough contest to judge. Every entry was like Marti's—personal, insightful, and moving. JoAnn ended up wanting a certain entry to win, and I wanted another. We solved our dilemma with the usual compromise: I told JoAnn we would go with her choice, and she insisted we go with mine. When we announced at the Christmas party that there would be two winners, I thought the excitement might overcome us all.

Joyce

Without revealing who picked whom, we will go alphabetically and start with Joyce.

Every time we take a new listing it goes to Joyce. Her role is to have the home staged, photographed, cleaned, repaired if necessary, and input onto the Multiple Listing Service. She oversees the file throughout the listing term. She juggles vendors, tradespeople, and agents. Clients love her; she is every seller's lifeline and knows all their preferences down to the smallest detail. This is how her entry began.

I didn't have any difficulty coming up with my examples of companies I have done business with that have put me first. They are the companies that I continue to do business with and that I still don't hesitate to refer my friends and family to. They are the ones that, when I reflect back, made a difference in my life. In some cases, they saved more than just the day.

My first example is my veterinarian. He is a mobile vet who has had his practice for many years. He treats not only house pets, but farm animals, too. He has a long list of longtime clients and he is very busy. It usually takes two to three weeks for him to get out to do simple immunizations, but the time that I had a sick pet he was there immediately. I had a kitty for about 10 years who suffered a sudden stroke. She went to the emergency clinic and stayed the entire night, but there was nothing they could do for her. I called Dr. Cahill in the morning after not sleeping the entire night, knowing I had to put my cat down. I was crying as I described her constant seizures to him and told him I couldn't stand to see it anymore and that I wanted her put down as soon as possible. He was there within a half hour.

After a few days, Brock told me I needed to go get a new cat to ease my sadness. I went to a no-kill shelter and adopted a new cat. She turned out to be ill and very nearly died in the first week that I had her. I'll never forget the visits from Dr. Cahill in the middle of the night to inject cold fluids under her skin to get her dangerously high fever down. One night, I called him at two o'clock in the morning and he came right over. If kitties count as clients, then Dr. Cahill definitely puts his clients first!

Joyce had several more examples that tugged at our hearts and spoke of caring and honesty, but it was her "clients last" story that resonated incompetence.

I was in an accident involving a driver who was driving a rented car. It was clearly his fault, and I had two unbiased witnesses who saw the accident and even stuck around and filled out a witness statement for the police. I really wanted to settle the claim with the rental car company, but they just kept dragging their feet. My car was not operable, and my car rental expenses were killing me. I had to submit the claim to my carrier and pay my $500 deductible to get my car fixed. My insurance carrier ended up settling for 80 percent of the damages from the rental car company, so I only got 80 percent of my deductible back. I was very upset, because I was not at fault in the least bit, so I called the adjuster at my insurance carrier. She explained to me that they had to settle, because there was no proof that we tried to stop to avoid the accident. I had her read the witness statements to me, where it asked the witnesses, "What brought our attention to the accident about to happen?" Both witnesses responded, "The guy in the car next to us slamming on his brakes." The insurance adjuster was caught and had to admit that she had settled for comparative negligence to get the claim off her desk. It was nice of my former insurance carrier to spend my money like that.

This lapse of diligence by the insurance adjuster was, to her, probably a minor blip in her day, but to Joyce it is a sore that can't be healed.

Sue

Our other cowinner was Sue. When clients initially call in about listing their homes, Sue takes the call. She listens and schedules a time for Kelly to see them. She does the research and prepares the listing. When Kelly comes back with the key, she prepares the file for Joyce. She also handles all the leases, goes on the occasional listing herself, and runs comps for appraisers so that our homes don't fall out of escrow. We've never had a client say an unkind word about Sue. She creates business and helps every agent on the team. Sue told us of her first job, a fortunate experience.

The company that I feel needs to be placed first on my list is Wegmans. It is a well-known name and household word to the people of Rochester, New York, and now to some neighboring states. Its philosophy is one of achieving incredible customer service, and it does this by first meeting the needs of its employees. I began working for this company when I turned 16, and even though people from out of state would refer to it as a grocery store, until you've been in one of these stores, it would be hard to imagine its scope. This company started out as a mom-and-pop store and grew into a company that has been ranked in the "100 Best Companies to Work For" nine times and has achieved the rank of number one and number two. With its 35,000 employees and 69 stores, its net sales in 2005 were $3.8 billion (I still follow its success). Wegmans also has a repertoire of other notable awards. Its stores are referred to as stores within stores and even draw tourists to view them.

What makes this company so important to me is that it started me out with lifelong lessons about the workforce and how things should be done to be successful. This company truly believes that customers should always be treated with respect and does what it takes to make them happy and keep them as lifetime customers, because every single person is important to the company. They do not squabble over anything. If a customer complains, it is fixed right there and then. They taught me how to deal with people and their needs and how something as simple as a replacement of a gallon of milk that went sour was an easy fix to keep a lifetime customer. They showed me that many times it was the small stuff that mattered to people and that if we listened, they would return.

As for taking care of their employees, that was a given. There were always little perks and bonus incentives to be had. There were summer picnics and Christmas parties. But most of all, there was the scholarship program. I received a four-year undergrad and two-year graduate school scholarship from this company. They would award employees after a rigorous application process with the condition that, during the time of scholarship, you would have to fulfill so many hours of employment per year. We received money for school, and Wegmans always had help—a win-win situation. I can credit them for getting me where I am today, because without them, I'm not sure how much college education I would have had. They made me want to work hard for them and always give my best. They were a company that placed value on education, and they showed it continually through the community and their business. I can proudly say my whole foundation for my work ethic has come from a company that lives by the meaning of *customers first*. You could say it is my foundation and my lifeline in the business world. I truly owe a great deal to them and have a warm fondness for them.

Sue went on to tell us about Disney, and both Sue and Joyce included comments in their entries about being a member of Those Callaways, a company they were proud to be a part of and a company they felt put the client first. The interesting thing is that this was long before JoAnn and I had discovered the three keys. We had not yet shared our story of that dark and stormy night when we realized that the only thing that mattered was keeping the client. The only thing our team knew was that our mission statement was just two words, *Clients First*, and that JoAnn and I lived it. They knew what they knew about "clients first" from their own personal experiences and from working with JoAnn and me.

Three Years Later

By Christmas 2009, we had discovered the three keys of *honesty*, *competence*, and *caring*, but we had not shared them with anyone. JoAnn and I were still testing our discovery. We were very hush-hush about the whole thing. Each night we would talk about the day and relate almost everything we did to the three keys. We questioned, we argued, we examined, and we worried that it was just too simple or that something was missing.

That Christmas, we had a contest similar to the one three years earlier. Without hinting at what we were looking for, we asked each agent on the team to name five ways they put clients first. Again, none of their answers directly recommended honesty. None of their responses espoused the virtue of competence. While there was a lot of caring, no one said what caring was or why we should care. Again, the three keys were between the lines.

Brian

Brian, who began years ago as our virtual tour agent and who now manages all of our bank portals, combines honesty with competence.

He said, "Trust is hard to earn and easy to lose. Confidence instills trust. From our very first contact, our confidence and belief in the team makes it easier for people to accept that what we're doing is real. That confidence is spawned from the trust each of us has for the team."

Brian also sees the simplicity of a two word mission statement. He said, "With *Clients First*, the most important principal is in the name—serving others. By understanding, by believing that fulfilling other's needs and by placing others ahead of oneself is the best way to actually fulfill your own needs, you quickly tap into a very powerful force in business."

Jeff

Jeff, our tech agent, had his own take on care. He said, "If there is anything that makes me feel as though I am getting first-rate service when I'm the customer, it's to know the provider is taking the time to hear what I'm saying. That also makes me feel as though I am a special customer and not just a walking wallet."

Alicia

Alicia, our contracts agent and youngest team member, recognizes the importance of competence. She said, "Our clients are confident in coming back to us and continually referring us to others because we know what we are doing. We are knowledgeable. We have a process for everything."

Aaron

Aaron, our marketing agent and art director, spoke of balance and momentum, but at the end he got to it. ". . . We need to be supportive and caring in these times most of all. That's when the ties that bind us are made. As the years roll on, people may not remember what we said, but they will always remember how we made them feel."

Joe

Our grandson, Joe, works for us as a short-sale agent. He found this quote by Sam Walton, the founder of Walmart. "There is only one boss. The customer. And he can fire everybody in the company from the chairman on down, simply by spending his money somewhere else."

These are wonderful people. But they are not unique or different from you. They have all the usual problems, misgivings, and insecurities we all have. They do a super job, yet they are not superhuman. They have become united under a simple two word mission statement: *Clients First.*

They each interpret its meaning in their own way, but they all *get it.* They are all honest with our clients. We trust them, and our clients trust them. They are all competent when serving our clients. If one person doesn't have an answer, another team member can help find it, so the client is well served. They all care deeply about our clients. JoAnn and I cried the first time we read these entries. We cry when we reread them. The caring shows through.

18 Trial by Fire

JoAnn and I didn't come home from Charlotte, write our nice little book, and live happily ever after. We came home to the worst real estate market crash since the Great Depression.

The early signs were there. This was the fall of 2006, and prices had leveled off for almost a year now. JoAnn kept pointing out the rising inventory of resale homes. By December, there were more than 55,000 homes for sale on our Multiple Listing Service system, and only 6,393 sold that month. At that rate, it would take nine months to sell the inventory.

Real Estate Had Been Changed Forever

In the spring of 2007, we heard that a mortgage company had closed its doors. By summer, several lenders had failed, and no-documentation loans were history. The median price of a Phoenix home had peaked at $262,000 a year earlier and was now down to $252,000. By September 2007, the credit crisis was in full swing, and more than 1,000 escrows canceled because the buyers no longer had financing. That December, there were almost 60,000 homes for sale, and only 3,318 sold, meaning the average seller could expect a sale in 18 months.

In 2008, prices tumbled, and we didn't see a bottom for 16 months. In January 2008, the median Phoenix home price was down to $235,000; by April 2009, it was half that ($117,500). During this slide, foreclosures flooded the market, and almost everyone agreed that the way you practice real estate had changed forever.

A Cash-Only Wasteland

This was devastating, not only to real estate agents, but also to everyone who relied on the real estate market. Title companies that earn fees based on the transactions alone and on the size of the transaction in dollars found themselves with massive reductions in cash flow. Business was down 50 to 75 percent, and many closed offices or dramatically cut staff, leaving one escrow officer to do the work of two or three.

Lenders were in full-scale panic. Offices closed. Names that had belonged to giants in the industry became fading memories. The credit crisis grew deeper and led to federal bailouts, beginning with the TARP funds and followed by many tweaks, as the government struggled to stimulate the economy. FHA-insured loans became the only vehicle available, and with its set limit, the market was immediately divided into two parts. The part that could get FHA financing grew to over 90 percent of the business, and the part that exceeded FHA loan limits became a cash-only wasteland, causing upper-class and luxury neighborhoods to suffer further.

No One Was Spared

Builders cut back to a few hundred housing starts each month in a metropolitan area that had demanded thousands of new homes in the past. All the trades, from carpenters to drywall installers, began to close down, move away, or search for remodeling work (which had diminished as well).

This contraction of the real estate activity was felt throughout the Arizona economy. No one was spared.

Dark Days

This was when we experienced another *Clients First* miracle. From that first night, when we decided to undo a deal we so desperately wanted to make, to the heights of the 2005 bubble, *Clients First* had been a two word miracle. It made everything easier. Our team believed in *Clients First*, and our business had grown exponentially. Our peers were in awe, often asking, "What is the real reason for your success?" But it wasn't until the dark days that we realized the power of these two words—*Clients First*.

Every morning the bad news would come over the fax, in the mail, via e-mail, or on the phone. A prominent lender committed suicide, reminiscent of the crash of 1929. A major real estate brokerage closed 14 offices. I personally heard of a once-successful agent selling blood to make her mortgage payment. Bankruptcies occurred everywhere. Custom builders were abandoning partially constructed homes.

Our Client Base Saved Us

Through it all, our gross commissions dropped less than 20 percent, whereas the market lost 70 percent of its dollar volume; ultimately, our income came back to 2006 levels while the overall market bottomed and stagnated. This was *Clients First* in action.

Every day the phone continued to ring. People continued to come to our open houses. Our client base saved us.

Did we make changes? Of course we did. But did we make basic changes? No. We continued to do business based on putting the client first and letting that be our guiding principle.

We Owed It to Our Clients

We continued to advertise our clients' properties even though the prevailing wisdom was that newspapers were dead and the only thing that moved real estate was price. We always believed we owed it to our sellers to maximize their homes' exposures in hopes of getting top dollar. Did we address price? Absolutely. In a falling market, you must keep your seller competitive or the property will languish unsold. We owed it to our clients to lay it on the line about price, and we did. We called every seller every week. We studied the comparable listings, pendings, and solds for each listing. We examined the showings and called for feedback. We asked for a price reduction, and when the home didn't sell in two weeks, we asked for another. This was imperative. Our sellers could not afford to chase the market. Our honesty kept our clients loyal. As other agents' listings expired, unsold, by the hundreds each week, and as hundreds more came on the market overpriced, we were able to sell our listings.

We actually increased our advertising by creating our own publication to showcase our listings. We called it *Callaway Country* and printed a new issue every three or four months. We created a unique delivery system for the magazine by placing a tube on each signpost. We refilled these tubes every week and showed our sellers how being advertised on 100 posts was better than being advertised on only the post in front of their home.

We invested in a new printer and improved our property flyers so our sellers would stand out even more. We did this in a falling market because our clients came first, and they had to compete as never before.

"Clients First" Rolled Off Their Tongues

These changes were a form of adapting to a changing real estate market, but the basic way we operated never changed. We never let anyone go and, for that matter, no one jumped ship. In fact, we grew our team by a few people to deal with the added intensity of dealing with a distressed market. The amazing thing is how little training these people required. We talked about *Clients First* when we interviewed them, and from day one these two words were the only training manual needed. Sure, we had to show them what the job was, but by the second day, "*Clients First*" rolled off their tongues like an old high school cheer.

This tremendous savings in time, effort, and money was unexpected. This was *Clients First* in action.

Real Estate Owned (REO)

As the market changed, so did the nature of the homes offered for sale. Up until the summer of 2007, a small portion, maybe 1 or 2 percent, of the market had been bank-owned or foreclosure properties. That began to change, and by the end of 2008, more than 70 percent of the homes sold each month were bank-owned, or REO properties. To ignore this segment of sellers would have been foolish, but how could we get these banks, a whole new kind of client, to call us?

We weren't the only agents to ask this question, and as the wave of foreclosures hit, a whole new group of agents emerged as market volume leaders. They were the old-time REO agents who for years had transacted a few deals each month for a bank or two where they had long-standing relationships. These agents were suddenly handling 100, 200, or 300 REO listings at one time. We had to get the bank clients or we would be left to survive on 30 percent of a market that now totaled half the dollar volume it had only two years before.

19 The Institutional Client

JoAnn didn't want to represent banks. She identified foreclosures, with all their misery and tragedy, and she wanted no part of them. No, we would take care of our clients and remain above the fray. If only our clients could make that choice as well.

The down market was affecting everyone. Stories of loss were everywhere. We had a choice to be part of the solution, or we could serve a vanishing market segment and disappear with it.

I Thought about It

Our resistance to change almost cost us everything. Because of our market leadership, we actually had three different banks come calling. We had been recommended by different local loan officers, and it was a golden opportunity. As JoAnn turned away the first bank, then the second, I thought about it.

I ran the numbers and found foreclosed properties selling in 30 days. I looked at the foreclosure notices filed with the county and saw them dramatically increasing. These notices gave homeowners 90 days before the bank took back the property. This meant that four or five months from now, the market would be flooded with real estate owned (REO) properties. This flood of homes would under-price the competition so they could be sold first. The rest of the market would go unsold. Our clients would have to compete or remain unsold. And if they wouldn't or couldn't compete, we would no longer, for all of our good intentions, be in business.

Our First Institutional Client

When the third bank sent a representative to us, I asked JoAnn to at least listen to what he had to say. This banker was visiting us because one of our clients managed one of the bank's mortgage offices. We had sold Kate's home and found the one she lived in currently. She knew our *Clients First* treatment personally, and she wanted very much to help us as well as her employer. She knew we would reflect well on her. The meeting went well, and we had our first institutional client.

Thus began a journey that would test *Clients First* as never before.

We called the other two banks and found that they weren't interested in coming back. Lesson one: Banks don't like to be told no. Dauntless as we are, JoAnn and I persevered. We called everyone. We asked for help. We wrote letters. At last, one of the loan officers who had recommended us in the first place went to bat for us and got us a second chance.

Lesson Two

Our folly did not end there. When we got our first property assignments from this bank, the homes were 30 miles away from our office, and they were nothing like our typical homes. Our primary market is northeast Phoenix, Scottsdale, and Paradise Valley. Our average sale was $400,000 to $500,000. These were homes on the edges of west Phoenix and they would sell for $50,000 to $60,000. The assignments come by e-mail, and we hit the reject button on the first four out of five. Our friend at the mortgage company, another past client, was mortified, and we learned lesson two: Banks *really* don't like being told no. It took us 18 months to get them past that but we did, thanks to *Clients First*.

Do Not Use

When the market began to change, there were maybe 10,000 REO agents in the country. That number quickly ballooned to 100,000 agents seeking REO work, and the banks quickly developed a one-strike policy. If you can't do the job, you get dropped, period. They mark your file DNU, which stands for Do Not Use, and it follows you no matter how many personnel changes occur at the bank.

The key with a no-margin-for-error new person in that position every week, "don't call me, use e-mail only client" is to be very competent and be very competent quickly. We had that one listing with that second bank, and we did the very best we could. We treated it like we treated any client's home. We cleaned it, photographed it, and created a virtual tour. We wrote a great description for MLS and produced a beautiful flyer. We advertised it and held open houses. No one had told us that many REO agents do none of these things, instead relying on a low price to do the job. We sold that house and fortunately got another. Eventually, we got more and more. We have this bank as a client today, thanks to our attitude of *Clients First*.

Keeping in Touch

We thought the third bank was lost to us until one day when JoAnn received a beautiful thank-you note from one of our clients whose home we had recently sold. He and his family had moved back to the Midwest. In his note, Charles referred some friends of his to us who were moving to Arizona from another state. Charles was on our mailing list thanks to JoAnn.

Since that first night that we resolved to put clients first, we have been committed to keeping in touch with our past clients. We mail Valentine cards and birthday greetings to them. At Christmas, we give them bread dough ornaments, which JoAnn designs and has hand-made during the year. We give Tiffany bowls, in the famous blue boxes, as gifts when we close on a property. We remember clients at Thanksgiving and Halloween and the Fourth of July. And when, after our first few years, I suggested we might economize and drop the folks who had moved out of state, JoAnn said no. Today, we mail gifts and cards to almost every state in the union and about a dozen foreign countries. You would be amazed at what it costs to send a Christmas ornament to Australia. You would also be amazed at how much business these far-flung clients send us each year.

Now He Wanted to Make Us First

JoAnn noticed that the postmark on Charles's note was a city that rang a bell. Wasn't this the headquarters for that other bank we had first turned down? In Arizona, Charles had been a mortgage banker, and his note mentioned that he had a new job at a bank. On the off chance there might be a connection, JoAnn called Charles and asked which bank. It was number three. She asked Charles whether he had anything to do with foreclosures (REOs), and Charles said no but that these people practically worked across the aisle from him. Would he find out who ran the REO department and write a letter for us? Of course he would. He was thrilled at the thought of helping us. *Clients First* had put Charles first, and now he wanted to do the same for us.

Here is the letter Charles wrote on our behalf. We have withheld the name of the bank and its headquarters to protect the privacy of the institution.

Dear [Key Executive],

I believe you may have recently received an REO REALTOR® submission package from JoAnn and Joseph Callaway located in Scottsdale, Arizona. I wanted to tell you a little bit about them, as I have had direct contact with both JoAnn and Joseph. We recently relocated back to [Midwest State] after 21 years in Scottsdale, Arizona. During that time I had the opportunity to work directly with JoAnn and Joseph and their entire team. I can tell you from firsthand experience that they are a top-notch professional team. My team of loan officers would constantly refer clients to the Callaways because of the work ethic they displayed. And when it came time to sell our home, we did not have to look far to find the best team.

The entire Callaway team brings a very professional approach to the real estate experience, both on the selling and listing side. They embody a full circle approach to the entire process and stop at nothing to go that extra mile to provide an experience that is sorely needed in today's marketplace. [Bank Name] would greatly benefit from this type of agent approach, especially in today's challenged markets.

It is rare that I give such recommendations, but when you experience excellence it must be noted. The Callaways will rise above your highest expectations!

Please feel free to call on me directly should you have any further questions about the Callaways.

Charles

Some might call this serendipity, a fortuitous coincidence, but we believe *Clients First* has a power to connect and reward its practitioners in miraculous ways. What are the odds of a far-flung past client going to work next to someone who could help save our business? That it happened stretches one's credulity. It is a prime example of how truth can sometimes be stranger than fiction.

We were approved in 30 days, and it was almost the death of us. This bank immediately assigned 20 properties to us—and a week later sent us 10 more. This wouldn't have been so bad, but other efforts had just culminated in another new bank sending 20 properties to us. Worse yet, we didn't know what we were doing. Each bank has its own system, rules, procedures, Internet portals, and timelines. These properties were spread all across central Arizona, and we had to become competent *right now*.

Very Good Very Fast

Our team, the team we put first, stepped up, regardless of what their traditional role had been. No one said, "That's not my job," or "I can't work that day." They all pitched in. Several nights, we didn't turn off the office lights until three o'clock in the morning. We became competent because that was what our clients expected. Competence was what we owed to our clients, and we became very good very fast.

Just think about it. Three clients, whom we had put first all those years ago, were now instrumental in our becoming REO agents at a time when only REO agents were thriving. Were it not for them, we might have had to downsize dramatically, saying good-bye to a wonderful team. Had we not been focused all those years on taking care of the client, no matter what the consequences, we might have had to do what so many agents did and find other work. It wasn't just these three clients who saved us—it was all those clients whom we had put first over the years. The fickle finger of fate chose these three, but only because it had so many from which to choose.

In this market, JoAnn and I have become walking encyclopedias on REOs and REO systems. We've attended conferences and conventions, joined organizations, and made personal connections with hundreds of agents and bank personnel. We added team members to handle the increased workload and devoted time to marketing our services to these institutional clients. We have treated their properties with the same level of care as we would the listing of our next-door neighbor. We have been honest with them in thousands of e-mails. We have learned what to do in every situation, and we have learned it well. In an industry with DNU files and one-strike rules, we haven't lost a single client. We deal with a new asset manager on almost every file, but we know our reputation is out there, and it is one of putting the client first.

We Can't Save the World, But . . .

What about all that tragedy and misery that JoAnn fought so hard to avoid? Working with banks and REO properties has put us on the front lines and given us an opportunity to help.

One day, an occupancy report came to JoAnn's desk, and the photographs showed a house full of furniture and toys and personal papers. This house was scheduled to be *trashed out* the next day by a third-party vendor hired by this particular bank. The required notices had been posted, and no one seemed to care that someone's life was still there.

JoAnn called the asset manager and asked for an extra day to try to find the former owner. She received permission, and we all went to work tracking down someone who didn't want to be found. This was made more difficult by privacy and liability considerations. We couldn't act like some paperback sleuth, nosing through unopened mail. There were clues, though. We could tell this was a woman with small children. From family photos, we knew she had been in the navy. From return addresses on envelopes, we found her parent in an eastern seaboard state. JoAnn called and explained the situation to this woman's mother and asked her to have her daughter call us. It was the best we could do. We could only hope that Mom believed JoAnn under circumstances that foster much disbelief.

We received the call late that night. This was a single mother who had no understanding of the foreclosure process. After seeing the notice on her door, she had fled the home. She was terrified that child protective services would come and take her babies because she had failed to pay her mortgage. She had moved to a rental house 50 miles away and was sleeping on the floor.

JoAnn turned to me and asked if we could help. My deal with JoAnn has always been that we can't save the world, but we can try to save the ones who cross our paths. I said yes. The next day, Jacie, our REO property presentation agent, met the movers, and by that night they finished loading. It was a full truck, and the day after that they made their delivery. The woman never called, but we know we eased her pain—and somewhere out there, we've made another karma deposit in the best bank of all, the *Clients First* bank.

20 The Distressed Client

G etting the institutional client to hire us and eventually rely on us because of our *Clients First* commitment was an important first step in dealing with a changing market. We couldn't be General Motors, selling big cars with the price of gasoline going through the roof. We had to mirror the market to stay in business, and if 70 percent of the homes for sale were bank owned, we needed to be selling them. Each month our business has reflected this overall market mix. In January of 2010, for example, the REO market was 39.5 percent of sales, and our REO business was 38 percent for that same month.

JoAnn and I also wanted to be part of the solution. We wouldn't be any good to our clients if we weren't around, and at the time we had no idea how deep the problem was. We thought if we would just help get these troubled assets through the system, we could all go back to the way things had always been.

Short Sales

Then Uncle Sam got involved. As foreclosures mounted, the government began a series of steps to stem the tide. The thinking in Washington was to take action before the banks ended up taking properties back. First came the foreclosure moratoriums. The next step was to address all those people in trouble by modifying their loans wherever possible. The government came up with the *home affordable modification program* (HAMP). Then the government came up with the *homes affordable foreclosure alternative* (HAFA). Short sales became the order of the day.

A short sale is a transaction in which the bank agrees to accept less than the balance owed so that a homeowner who cannot keep paying the mortgage may have a more respectable outcome than foreclosure.

Up to now, JoAnn and I had dealt with regular clients. Sure, they came in all sizes and shapes, but they had normal motivations. Even the banks just wanted their foreclosed properties to be sold. The short sale created a whole new kind of client, the distressed seller, with all that the situation entailed.

Clients First Tested Again

A rapidly falling market is a terrible thing. With every percentage point drop in prices, wealth vanishes. It doesn't matter whether we're talking about stocks, real estate, business inventory, or Grandpa's coin collection, the value drops. Equity drops. You don't even have to sell at the lower price to feel the effect. You feel less rich, poorer, and insecure.

Those who desperately want to sell or refinance feel the loss. Homeowners who think their home's equity would be a resource for retirement or putting the kids through college suddenly don't have a plan. The loss runs deep, and it takes an emotional toll.

With the changing market, our clients changed. They became afraid. With their fear came anger, remorse, denial, mourning, and dozens of other negative emotions that can be lumped into one word: *distress*. People in the market became contentious and full of doubt. Buyers were no better off than sellers. They worried that buying too soon would cause them an immediate loss if the market tumbled further.

Adapt and Survive

In a falling market, businesses fail or cut back, stripping themselves of their most precious asset: good people who can make their business succeed. JoAnn and I saw this all around us. Early on, we considered cutting back. We could hole up until the firestorm passed. But what would we have when the sun came out? We could not put our clients first and retreat at the same time. Although many business leaders fold up their tents and steal away with no effect on those who are left behind, in some crazy way we felt our clients needed us. Our deliberations were short-lived, and we committed to adaptation and survival.

Lessons, Lessons, Lessons

We learned a lot from the falling market. We learned that clients *did* need us. They needed someone who would be honest with them. When clients are distressed they need the truth. Kidding them, or supporting people who are kidding themselves, can be devastatingly costly. As the market slid and each sale hit a new low, we worried about what we had cost our clients. Then, as the market slid further, we would look back a few months later and be glad we had saved those clients when we did.

We learned the value of competence as we observed negligence all around us. We invested anew our time and energy to be the best, to be on the cutting edge as things changed. Real estate had become ever more affected by government and legal considerations. We had to redouble our efforts to remain competent.

A distressed market brings with it despondence and ambivalence. We found ourselves caring about clients who had stopped caring. They didn't care whether the bank lost money. They didn't care whether the buyer got a house in sound condition. They blamed the government, the financial institutions, their neighbors, and themselves. We had to deal with their grief, anger, and remorse. But we *cared*, and many times our caring saved clients from their despair. *Clients First* saved us, and it saved them.

If You Don't Have to, Don't

As the market went into free fall, we tried to get our sellers' homes sold, but in many cases they ran out of equity before a buyer could be found. As prices dropped further, they became more *upside down*, owing more on their mortgage than their home could possibly sell for. They didn't have any equity, and the question was what to do.

Dozens of times each day, JoAnn and I would advise, "If you don't have to sell, don't." We told clients that this was no time to sell if you didn't have to, but we found many who *did* have to sell. They had lost income, got divorced, or needed to move out of state. They were distressed. Some clients had to buy. If you have three big dogs or five children or four cars, it's not easy to find a rental. They had to buy in a falling market, and they were afraid. These buyers needed to be put first. They needed honesty, competence, and care.

Disbelief Was the Order of the Day

We saw a new side to the lending community as well. Banks were losing a ton of money, and they didn't want to face it. Short sales are handled by a separate department, called *loss mitigation*. Unlike asset managers who want to get REO properties off the bank's books, loss mitigators were just like our distressed clients. They saw everything in negative terms and fought the process every step of the way. After all, until the property is sold short or taken back in foreclosure, the loan is still on the books. Disbelief was the order of the day, and the bankers questioned everything. The lenders were in distress.

Short sales grew to 35 percent of the homes for sale, and REOs retreated to 35 percent. It was still a 70 percent bank-controlled market, but the distress meter was off the chart.

We Added Clients

Again, *Clients First* played a vital role. As this whole short sale scene evolved, our honesty, competence, and care showed through. We justified our values with extensive market comparables so the banks could have confidence in what we told them. Every day, we improved our short sale package so that our client's file would have the best chance. We took every class, attended every convention. We stayed on the cutting edge. We cared about and for our clients, and they in turn stayed with us.

Clients First got us through the distress. We didn't cut back. We actually added to the team. We didn't offer less. We offered more. We didn't lose clients. We added to our client list. Every buyer who bought one of our bank properties, every buyer who bought one of our short sales, and every buyer who bought one of our traditional resales became a client of Those Callaways. We treated them and their agents with the same honesty, competence, and care—and when they are ready to sell in the future, they will call us. Every seller who sells with us is a current or future buyer. We keep in touch with them all. We know that *Clients First* will bring them all back. They bring their friends and their families to us, and we will serve them again and again.

Every Day, the Phone Rings

Those Callaways has survived challenge after challenge, market change after market change, ups and downs. *Clients First* has guided us and inspired us through it all. Every day, when we answer the phone, it is a past client bringing us new business. Every day, we again commit to putting our *Clients First*, no matter what the consequences; and every day, we are thankful for that moment driving north on 71st Street with rain on the windshield and enlightenment in our hearts.

Clients First will take you wherever you want to go, and along the way, *Clients First* will be your spare tire and your auto club card, making sure you get there. It is easy to say, "Look at what we did; look how we succeeded in real estate." But it is a miracle that we survived and thrived in the real estate crash. It is a miracle, a *Clients First* miracle, that can be yours as well.

Why Number One?

JoAnn and I travel a lot, and we've figured out that at least 36 states have car dealerships that claim to be "the number one automobile dealer in the world." The only reason dealers in the other 14 states don't make that claim is because it would be hard for North Dakotans to believe they had enough people to substantiate it, even if every man, woman, child, and dog bought an SUV each year. Why do these car agencies promote market leadership? All sorts of business owners like to say they are number one. Real estate agents do it all the time. What doctor would not want the title of number one heart surgeon in the world? I'm sure the answers are many and the reasons lengthy. These titles certainly stroke the egos of the owners and make employees feel proud. But how meaningful are they to the client?

I remember a story about two gentlemen observing the foot traffic outside Macy's department store in New York. The first asked, "Why do so many people shop at Macy's?" The second gentleman gave it some thought and replied, "I guess it's because so many people shop at Macy's."

May As Well Close the Doors

So, does it matter?

Not everybody can be number one, and those who can't often downplay the importance of what they cannot achieve. They say,

"I don't want to be the biggest. I just want to be the best." Or they downplay it further by saying they just want do a good job or just have enough to make a good living.

JoAnn has told thousands of clients, "It doesn't matter how many homes we've sold. It only matters that we sell *yours*." She has done this even though we have been the market leaders for years. We've never put the claim in an ad. We don't tell everyone we meet. But is it important to JoAnn? You bet. She knows that we are either number one with our clients or else we may as well close the doors.

Customers act on their first choices; if that choice is unavailable, an individual makes a new first choice. Customers work with their first choices 100 percent of the time.

Two Is the Road to Failure

Being number one in your industry, field, area, sport, or niche is vital. The best job security is being the best employee. If you want to be the last person standing in a downsizing, then you want to offer the best value to your employer. The boss is, after all, your client. Striving to be less, to give less, only makes you vulnerable. Number two is the road to failure.

A lot of people know we are number one without us saying anything. Our staff knows it. Other agents know it. Title companies and lenders know. Many of our clients know. Some are pleasantly surprised when they find out. I think they like it. They are a little like the Macy's customers. There is a comfort in knowing their choice is shared by others, but in the end, JoAnn is right. All that matters is that we sell their house, take care of them.

I guess the question is, can we just take care of that client and his or her one house if we are striving for mediocrity? Can we really be the best if we are not trying to be number one? Isn't that what number one signifies?

Clients First Makes Us Competitive

Number one implies a competition. Being number one says you are a winner. Looking back, the question posed by the lady in blue at the

Mustang Library has a larger answer. She asked JoAnn, "But what is the *real* secret of your success?" This haunted us for years, because we didn't know how to explain *Clients First*. Today, we have the answer and even more.

Putting *Clients First* makes us competitive. At any given time, there are anywhere from 20,000 to 60,000 homes on the market in Maricopa County. If we are to care about getting that one client's home sold, we must make it the first choice of a buyer who has all those other homes from which to choose. We must compete. *Clients First* demands it. We must make our client's home number one.

When our buyer wants to make an offer on a home after looking at 70 houses, and we call the other agent only to find out there are three other offers, we must compete. We must position our buyer to be number one with that seller.

Caring about a client's ambitions puts us in a contest to fulfill his or her dreams. If we are going to win, we must be good at what we do. We must be competent. If we are to win, it must be an honest victory. *Clients First* is all about winning. It is all about being number one. It's all about making your client number one. You cannot truly be number one until your clients are.

Like a Religious Experience

We met with a client one Monday morning, and he was excited to have an offer on his home, but he was even more excited about the weekend he had just experienced. He had just returned from Wisconsin, where he met his fiancée, and they attended a football game in Green Bay. I get a chill when I think about it. He described going to Lambeau Field. He said it was like a religious experience, and now, 24 hours later, he was still on a high that infected all of us at the table.

I've thought about that morning a number of times since. JoAnn and I are not Green Bay fans. We live in Arizona and root for the Cardinals. Yet we were caught up in this client's excitement for a team more than 1,000 miles away. I don't even recall whether the Packers won the game. What I remember was how the Packers make their fans feel.

Professional football is about competition in one of its purer forms. The NFL is populated with competitors, from the front office to the field. They are all driven personalities. They all want to win. They all want to be number one. But whom do today's superstars play for? Do they play for themselves, or do they play for their fans? After all, their clients are their fans, but how many of them know that?

How many other teams have fans like those in tiny Green Bay, Wisconsin? By all standards, Green Bay shouldn't even have a team. They have no metropolitan media market. They exist only because they go back to a time before television and mass merchandising. Yet they are filling the stands week after week and leaving their fans breathless—win or lose. Some big cities can't even sell all the seats in their new stadiums. The Los Angeles market is 20 million people strong, and they can't get a team. But tiny Green Bay serves its clients and puts them first. The Green Bay Packers not only survive, they thrive. Green Bay has fans all over the world. How many other franchises can make that claim?

She Had Drive and Determination

JoAnn and I have always been competitive. One time, when we were in our 30s and vacationing, the resort where we stayed had a badminton net set up on the lawn. Having nothing else to do, we picked up the rackets and began tapping the shuttlecock back and forth. Three hours later, we quit—and the next day we were both so stiff we couldn't get out of bed until dinner. We can be very driven.

But it was not until the night we decided to put *Clients First* that our drive had power. Up until that night, we were like so many people. Our drive to succeed was directed inward. We wanted to win for ourselves. I knew from the look in her eye that the woman at the Mustang Library wanted very much to succeed. She had drive and determination. She also had 20 years in the business, and she was still searching for the real secret to success. We tried to tell her, but we failed, because we didn't know how to tell her at that time.

If she's still out there and reading this book, let me answer her now: "Put your *Clients First*, and put all that drive and ambition into delivering to them what they want."

When you put your *Clients First*, you channel your spirit through them. Their success becomes your success. Strive to make them number one. Win for them; when you do, you will achieve as never before, and your victories will be rich. You can't be number one until your clients are, but when you exalt them, they will lift you up on their shoulders and chant your name as they carry you from the field.

22 Going Forward

Bob Dole lost his bid for the White House in less than 10 seconds. It was during his presidential debate with Bill Clinton. He was practiced, poised, and a respected senator. He had his party's nomination and was admired by many. But he was older than Clinton, and he wanted a way to express the value of his wisdom. Perhaps he hadn't thought it through, or perhaps one of his staffers hadn't considered the ramifications, when Dole said, "I want to be a bridge to the past."

In what seemed like a nanosecond, Clinton quipped, "Well, I want to be a bridge to the future," and it was over. Oh, they had to go on for a few more weeks, money had to be spent, polls had to be taken, an election had to be held, but it was over. Bob Dole lost because Bill Clinton had a quick comeback and used Dole's own incomplete thought against him.

I believe Dole's argument, although he never got to make it, was that there is value in looking at the past as long as we learn from it. With age comes wisdom from the accumulation of past experiences. Would Bob Dole have been a better choice for the American people? We will never know. It looks as if history will be more than kind to Bill Clinton, who was a great president, but Dole lost it all in an ill-advised nine words.

We Had No Idea

As we go forward, we cannot help but look at the past. As we examine our *Clients First* experience, as we look for clues to verify the three keys, as we try to prove our work, we find ourselves overwhelmed with the goodwill that *Clients First* has created. Could we have created the same branding with less care and more flash? Could we have been less competent and satisfied our clients as well? Could we have spun the truth to meet our own needs and held the confidence of 5,000 clients? I don't believe so.

The more JoAnn and I look at where we are and where we came from, the more we shake our heads in disbelief. We did not expect this. We weren't used to winning. When *Clients First* came to us that night as we were driving north on 71st Street in the rain, we had no idea what it would bring.

Every Day Is Special

We had our hopes and dreams. They were vague and changed often. One day, JoAnn and I fantasized about owning a small shopping center. We would have a bookstore, a flower shop, a gift shop, a breakfast joint—all the things we love under one long roof. We don't want it now, but it was a special moment and a precious memory. Today, we dream of world travel and organizing our family photos. Who knows what we will do going forward, but whatever we do will be powered by our *Clients First* experience.

One of the greatest gifts of *Clients First* is a confidence that all will turn out right. *Clients First* allows us to enjoy each moment, each client, each day. We sleep well each night. We know that whichever way the real estate market goes, we will go with it. We will stay competent. We will adapt and learn and upgrade our technology. We will care and be rewarded with joy. We know this, and it makes every day special.

Looking back, I realize that JoAnn and I are not the same people we were that morning when we struggled to explain our change of heart to Marta and Susan. *Clients First* changed us. It changed our capacity for work. It changed our ability to envision a bigger picture.

It changed our comprehension of money. It made us more understanding, compassionate, and humble.

Have we proven our work? Have we made a case for *Clients First* and the three keys? Remember, you have to be the judge and jury. We believe we have. Everything we have done, all our accomplishments, our team, our fellow agents, our corporate family, and our thousands of clients tell us that we are correct.

They Never Get It

It seems so simple. That's what really scared us. Can the real secret be so obvious? And, if it is there for all to see, how can it still be a secret? Yet it is, because so few seem to know. People go on thinking that the truth is what they want it to be and that they can fake it until they make it and that the only one they should care about is number one. They go through life stumbling all around *Clients First* and never *get it*. We sincerely hope that you stub your toe on this marvelous secret, and maybe, just maybe, it will change your future.

Every day we are thankful for the gift of *Clients First*. It has made all the difference for us, so we wish to pass it on to you. We want you to have your own *Clients First* experience.

Are You Ready?

You cannot imagine the changes *Clients First* will bring to your life. You cannot plan it (not that there is anything wrong with goals and dreams). You should know where you want to go. You should have a picture in your mind of your destination. Otherwise, how will you know which road to take? But when you fill your personal tank with *Clients First*, you will find your trip supercharged. You will find yourself going faster than you ever thought possible. You will find shortcuts and beautiful scenic overlooks. Your journey will be the reward, and each time you achieve and reach your destination, you will find a new one to take its place. With *Clients First*, you will know you can make it.

Are you ready to begin your journey?

How to Put Your *Clients First*

The Path to *Clients First*

"**B**ut tell me," she said, "what's the *real* reason for your success?" That question haunted JoAnn and me. We kept telling people that putting *Clients First* was the reason, and they kept saying, "Sure, uh-huh," and then they would drift away with an unsatisfied look on their faces that said they just knew that we were holding back or hiding something. We were keeping a secret, the real secret to success.

Gradually, the questions began to change. I guess enough people had heard our story enough times that they began to think we might just be telling the truth as we saw it and that maybe, just maybe, there might be something to this *Clients First* thing. Then they would ask, "But how? How do you put *Clients First*?" Sometimes I think we just traded one unanswerable question for another. Or maybe that should be one questionable answer for another.

To be fair, we might just be a couple of ambitious folks who got lucky. If you were to question our clients, they might say they come to us because of our marketing, or because so-and-so recommended us, or because JoAnn is such a good dealmaker. They might say we make them feel good. They might even say we put them first, but most likely they won't say that. If you ask other agents, they might offer anything from how nice we are on the phone to some grumbling complaint of inequity born out of their own competitive spirit.

They certainly wouldn't latch on to the idea that we treat our clients better. Most agents feel they do a good job for their clients, and often this is very true.

Perhaps it was just a fortuitous time to enter real estate, but we've already pointed out that in 1997, interest rates were almost 9 percent, and nothing about the prior 16 years would have recommended real estate as a vocation. We have since survived a bubble and a crash and managed to prosper through both. People who enter real estate today have the same opportunity we did. The future surely holds another bubble and another crash, although I wouldn't wish for either. Cycles are simply a reality of economics.

You Need a Plan

If *Clients First* really is the secret of our success, and we believe it is, then how does someone do it? How do you put *Clients First* into action? What do you do today? What do you do tomorrow? How do you transform your business, job, department, or corporation into a *Clients First* enterprise? You need a plan.

JoAnn and I didn't have a plan. We didn't choose *Clients First*, it chose us. Our miracle was a transformation. We are not the same two kids who entered real estate halfway through their lives. *Clients First* changed us in fundamental ways. Looking back, it was both gradual and sudden.

Some time ago, a fellow agent spoke about the mystery of change. He said that you gradually stop paying attention to your profit and loss statements, and then suddenly you are broke. You gradually let things slide with employees, and suddenly you have a do-nothing workforce. You gradually lose appreciation for your spouse, and suddenly you are divorced. Likewise, it would be unrealistic to expect sudden success without a gradual progression toward that success.

You Need a Path

JoAnn and I had no destination in mind that night when we decided to put our *Clients First*. We didn't know where this enlightenment would lead us. It just took hold of us and wouldn't let go. Perhaps our story will do the same for you: grab you, haunt you, and not let you slip away. But you still need a plan and a destination. You need a path to walk and steps to take. You need to know how to put *Clients First*.

Coming up with what happened to us has been a reconstructive effort. Like a crime scene investigator, we had to look for evidence and clues and try to figure out what transpired. Which events led up to *Clients First*, and which events followed? What was the sequence, and could it or should it be duplicated? Was our path the only one? You are an individual, and your plan should be yours alone.

What we did discover was a natural progression dictated by *Clients First*. There were events and steps that followed one another as a result of our decision to put *Clients First*. We saw how we had followed this evolution. We could relate to each change as it came in succession. We examined the reasons, and when we were satisfied we came up with a list of steps. As you apply these to your own situation, you will find some steps require longer strides than others. Then again, what may be a short step for you might be the longest stretch of all for another. You have to accept that you must make these steps your own. You need to internalize each of them to your own experience. But complete them you must. Each of these steps is necessary. Don't be tempted to take shortcuts. *Clients First* will be there for you in the end. You want to be completely ready for it when you arrive.

The Path to *Clients First*

Step 1: Make the commitment.
Step 2: Speak the commitment.
Step 3: Keep the commitment.
Step 4: Get yourself out of the way.
Step 5: Set the monkey down.
Step 6: Put your faith in others.
Step 7: Trust the truth.
Step 8: Allow the work to be the reward.

Step 9: Learn to like people.
Step 10: Turn it around.
Step 11: Give to get.

As we guide you along this path, we share the changes we experienced and offer suggestions regarding how you may make similar changes. There is no timetable. But our hope is that your transformation has already begun.

A Change Within

Remember that *Clients First* is not a department, division, or position. It's not candy or balloons or cookies from home. It's not frequent-flyer miles or customer-affinity programs. It's not regularly scheduled contacts to ask for referrals. And it is not memorized patter designed to up-sell a customer's dinner selection. *Clients First* is not a campaign precipitated on the company's human resources so that they may be more relationship focused. No, it is not a trendy methodology of the day designed to uplift and inspire for as long as its luster can shine. *Clients First* is a change within you.

Clients First is a mind-set, a commitment, a fundamental change that does not go away in a year, a month, or a day. *Clients First* is real. It comes from the spirit and the heart of the individual. *Clients First* is a personal exchange between two people. It cannot be packaged or bottled. It cannot be conferred on the organization from the executive suite.

If you are looking for *Clients First* in a poster or a company memo or a broadcast e-mail, you can save yourself the time and effort. *Clients First* is not an outward thing; it is an inward change. If you want to make that change and benefit from the bounty offered by *Clients First*, then you must look inside yourself for the answers.

The answers will be personal. The change will be uniquely yours. You will change on your own terms. JoAnn and I can only share what happened to us, and from that personal experience we can offer to you a map, a path that only you can walk. We promise you it is a path to wondrous things. *Clients First* is a trip worth taking.

Step 1

Make the Commitment

When JoAnn and I discovered *Clients First* for ourselves, it was instantaneous, transformational, and life changing. It came with a single turn of a phrase. Faced with making a deal that was't right for our clients, JoAnn said, "Why don't we undo it all?" I immediately knew the rightness of her words. It was as clear as my vision became when I put on prescription glasses for the first time after years of denial and thinking I could see just fine.

Your moment may come just as quickly, or it may be a gradual realization. This will be up to you, but it is the beginning. It is the first step along the path to *Clients First*.

Fear and Resentment

When I was a young man, most of my friends and I had a fear of commitment. We were afraid of being locked in, so when asked about what we wanted to do with our lives or what our college major would be, we would cling to "undecided" as if it would protect us a while longer. We feared growing up. We feared responsibility. What I didn't realize then was that I really *had* made commitments. I was committed to football in the fall and track in the spring and kissing a girl in the summer. These were worthy endeavors for a boy of 15.

As I grew up, as I took on responsibility, I found myself swamped with commitments, many of which came with a statement once a month. Every time I said yes, I formed a new commitment. *Yes, I'll come in to work on Sunday. Yes, we'll help with the school fund-raiser. Yes, we'll buy a new couch.* Every now and then, I would melt down because of having too much to do, and I would pull back, only to gradually commit to new things. I resented commitment.

JoAnn's experience is uniquely her own, but she admits to times she feared or resented commitment. If you look into your own heart, you have probably felt the same thing. Commitments can be oppressive masters and should not be taken lightly.

An Uncommitted Life

Of course, commitments are not all bad. Some commitments lead to wonderful things. A committed relationship, a good marriage, a lifelong partnership—these things bring a reward to the spirit unattainable otherwise. All great things happen as a result of commitment. We committed to the defeat of Hitler and won World War II. We committed to little more than a halfhearted resistance to Communism in Vietnam, and that war is today a scar on our nation. James Cameron committed more money than had ever been spent on making a movie and gave us *Avatar.* JoAnn and I committed to each other and found lifelong joy.

Can we lead an uncommitted life? Yes. Will it lead to greatness? No.

As we finally gain maturity, we learn to embrace commitment, for without it we simply stumble through an uncommitted life filled with small memories. We must put away childish things and step up. We must take a stand, make a decision, and commit ourselves to something, or else we will have to live with the consequences of never having done so.

Say Yes

Is *Clients First* a worthy commitment? Will *Clients First* lead to greatness? We believe it is and it does. Deciding to pursue the goal of putting your *Clients First* is the right thing to do. It is a worthy pursuit, and it will reward you greatly.

How do you make a commitment to putting *Clients First*? You say yes.

Would you rather say no? Do you think it would be better to go on ignoring your clients? Should you stick with business plans that refer to revenue sources rather than customers? Do you want to keep tinkering with business models that attempt to respond to market metrics and enhanced competitive position? Or would you be better off saying yes to taking care of your customers first.

It is a simple question. Yes or no?

Careful Consideration

Before you say yes, you should think about this. A quick yes could lead to a shallow commitment. You'd be better off with no commitment than one that has no depth. Your yes, if that is what you decide, should be a resounding *yes*. Your yes should well up from within you like a fountain, and you should shout it out. This is the commitment that lasts. This is the commitment *with legs*.

We suggest you examine the no option carefully. The no has served you fine this far. You may consider yourself fortunate. You may have already achieved the success you seek. You may be satisfied with the way things are. You may have never cared about your customers one way or the other and succeeded anyway. Maybe you delegated caring about your clients. Think about this carefully. The difference between commitment and no commitment is simply the difference between yes and no.

Don't Be an Easy Yes

Some business coaches and business books recommend that, for life balance, you are better off learning how to say no, and we could not agree more. A strong no is often a kindness to yourself and others. Overcommitment can be a killer. It can bring stress and burnout. You don't want to be an easy yes.

And we don't want an easy yes. We want your yes to be made with your eyes wide open. *Clients First* will change you. It will change the way you think and interact with people. *Clients First* is not a part-time avocation. You cannot be putting your *Clients First* one moment and then forget about them the next. *Clients First* is all-in, a total immersion.

Why, you might ask, are we making this so hard? If *Clients First* is so good, why not make it easy? Good question. You see, it is not that *Clients First* is easy; it is that *Clients First* makes everything else easy. Deciding to put our *Clients First* at all times goes against the grain of much that we do. Most of our lives are about ourselves, and through selfish decisions we seek short-term easy and trade it for long-term hard. JoAnn and I were like that. We took care of each other and our families and not much else. We were passionately patriotic and had opinions on anything and everything. We thought of ourselves as quiet neighbors and good citizens. But we didn't have a clue about helping others. We helped when asked. We gave to charities. We were happy.

Welcome to a Miracle

Then we said yes to *Clients First* and everything changed. We changed. Yet we are still quiet neighbors. We still take care of ourselves and our family, but now our clients take care of us as well. Did this create a short-term hardship? Surprisingly, we simply traded the short-term ease of selfishness for what has become the short-term ease of *Clients First*. The more we give, the more we receive, because what we give is *Clients First*.

How do you make the commitment to *Clients First*? You say yes.

If this is your decision, and yours alone, welcome to a miracle. Welcome to *Clients First*. You have taken step number one and made the commitment. Your life has begun to change. Now you must take the next step.

25

Step 2

Speak the Commitment

That next morning, JoAnn and I shared our discovery with Susan and Marta. We spoke of our new commitment to *Clients First*. We made it real by talking to the girls and each other about doing what is best for the client.

This is the second step you will take on the path to *Clients First*. Once you have made your commitment, you must share it with others. You must *speak* your commitment, for this will make it real.

Embarrassment

Me and my big mouth—could I ever get myself in trouble! All the times I could have just kept my mouth shut, but no, I just had to speak up. I had to tell someone what I thought. I had to express my opinion. I had to set someone straight. It is so embarrassing to look back on all the dumb things I said when I could have said nothing.

My mother used to tell me, "The kindest thing to do and say is the kindest thing in the kindest way." I would say, "Sure, Mom," and then go out in the world and blow it.

JoAnn was better than me about this. Of course, I think she is better than me in almost every way. I can open a pickle jar for her, but that's about where my male supremacy ends. JoAnn was always more diplomatic, more tactful, and yes, more kind. But she had her moments, and they were doozies. Afterward, she would blame me for not stopping her—as if I could halt a locomotive by standing on the track! No, we weren't perfect. We are not today. But today, I think my mom would be proud of me.

Positive and Negative

I remember a story about two men standing by a fence talking. The one man was a contractor paving the road next to the fence. He had stopped to take a break. The other was the farmer who owned the field on his side of the fence, and he just liked to make friends. As they talked, they heard thunder in the east and, when they looked, could see dark clouds advancing toward them. The farmer smiled, because his crops needed the rain; the contractor frowned, because he would lose a day's work and needed the money for his family. The rain was a single event, but it was both a positive (for the farmer) and a negative (for the road builder).

There is scientific theory that proposes that all things have both a positive and a negative charge. Money can be used for good and it can be used for evil. Religion can bring peace or cause strife. You can associate with the right people or you can fall in with the wrong crowd. All these things can be positive or negative. Likewise when you open your mouth.

Your words have the power to lift and the power to destroy.

You Have a Choice

You can build your children up or you can tear them down. You can tell your spouse you love him or her or you can find fault at every turn. You can say the kindest thing in the kindest way or you can be a critical hellion. It is a choice we make, and we do our best, but we don't always choose well.

Thank goodness no one hears every word you say. You can be careful around certain people. Your boss may never hear a profanity from your lips, while your best friend might know you as a potty mouth. That's how we do it. We gauge what we say, when we say it, and to whom we are speaking. No one hears it all. But then, that's not exactly true.

One person does hear every word. That person is you. You hear it all. Sometimes you are pleased with yourself and sometimes you embarrass yourself, but there is no escaping the fact that you hear it all.

Just as the words you speak to others can please or shame, the words you speak to yourself have the power to lift you up or tear you down. Again, the decision is yours. You can choose what you say or don't say. You have the power to speak your commitment to putting *Clients First* or you can say nothing.

Making It Real

If you speak your commitment, if you tell others of your intention to put *Clients First*, you will find that your words strengthen your commitment. If you say nothing, your commitment begins to wither like a flower without water.

JoAnn and I spoke that morning to our small two-person staff about our experience the night before, and it was like a one-two punch—bam that night and bam that morning. Speaking our commitment to *Clients First* made it real.

Weight Watchers made a fortune on this one thing: If you diet and speak your commitment to others once a week, then you will lose weight. Alcoholics go to meetings to speak their commitment to another day without drink. Corporations have their retreats so they can speak their commitments to the company's goals.

This is the next step, and you must take it. If you do not speak your commitment, you will allow yourself to wander off the path, where you may stumble and fall. Not speaking your commitment to *Clients First* is like asking yourself to be superhuman, because the energy required will be tenfold. Committing is hard enough as it is. Speaking your commitment gives you strength.

Speaking your commitment will make it stronger. Each time you tell someone that it is your goal to put your clients first, they will think more highly of you and you will think more highly of yourself.

JoAnn and I say it all the time. We've come up with dozens of variations. We say to the client, "What we want is whatever is best for you." We say our goal is to serve their best interest. We tell them we have a two word mission statement, and it is *Clients First*.

Our teammates speak the commitment as well, although I don't think they ever think of it that way. They probably don't even know they made a commitment. They just join Those Callaways, and we all talk about how nothing else matters as long as we take care of the client, and they fall into it, and pretty soon they are saying the words and acting the part, and, wow, they are putting *Clients First*.

Just Say "Next"

You might find it awkward at first. You might tell someone that you have decided to put *Clients First*, and they may react in any number of ways, some of them negative. Just remember the farmer and the paving contractor. Everything has a plus and a minus. If someone responds in a negative fashion, just let it slide.

Late-night television host David Letterman often reads jokes from index cards. Sometimes they get laughs and sometimes they die. When that happens, David flicks the card off into the backdrop of the television set as though to say, "Next." David uses this flicking gesture to protect himself from rejection. If some people don't just fall all over themselves with admiration for your new commitment to putting *Clients First*, say, "Next" and move on.

I've had people say things like, "I would hope so," or "Of course you should." They might think I'm stating the obvious. But the obvious often needs restating. Don't be afraid to speak your commitment. It is for *you* that you do it, and for the most part it will receive a positive response. To let those negative people so pompously dismiss your commitment is to let the forces of evil steal your passion.

Be passionate. Be unrepentant. Be bold. Speak your commitment and claim your reward.

And remember to keep speaking your commitment. *Clients First* is not for just a day, a week, or a month. It is for always, which brings us to our next step.

Step 3

Keep the Commitment

Since that night and the morning after, *Clients First* has changed our lives, but we are human, with all the frailties that come with being mortal. We have fallen down and had to pull each other up. As powerful as *Clients First* is, we have struggled with its execution. As strong as our commitment is, we have had to guard against slipping back into the people we were before.

Keeping the commitment is your third step along the path to *Clients First*. Again, just as we found our own solutions, you will have to find the tools that work for you. We offer suggestions, but you must do the work.

Heroes

One day, I explained to JoAnn that she was my hero. She had just made a deal for a client that to anyone else would have seemed impossible. The negotiation had gone on for weeks. They started impossibly far apart. There was every reason to give up, but JoAnn never did. She just kept going, like a dachshund with a leather chew toy bigger than herself. Eventually, the last of the obstacles succumbed to her determination, and our client was rewarded. She thanked me when she heard my hero comment, and I said, *"No, you don't understand."*

"Let me explain what I mean," I said. "You see, a hero is usually defined in a story as the protagonist, the one for whom the audience roots. But what really makes that person the *hero* is all the people around her urging her to give up. The best friend says, '*I hate to see you do this to yourself.*' The boss says, '*It can't be done.*' The kids say, '*We are being neglected.*' And the villain seems undefeatable. The worse the villain, the greater the obstacles, and the louder the naysayers, the greater the hero becomes."

I continued, "*That* is what a hero is, and that is why I say you are my hero."

JoAnn cried when I told her that. I don't know whether it was the emotional relief from making the deal or because she loves me so much, but we will both remember it forever.

You can be a hero, too. Just never give up.

Get Back Up

I've gained and lost hundreds of pounds. I'm on a diet today. I might be overweight, but I haven't given up and ballooned to something the size of Chicago. I'll keep on, and someday I'll be the right weight and stay there. Of course, I'll never weigh what the doctor's chart says I should, but that's denial rather than giving up.

We've been broke, but we've never been poor. My grandparents thought of themselves as poor. They lived through the Great Depression and revered President Roosevelt. They were proud and afraid. They had been unable to pay one bill in 1944, and for the next 30 years they never applied for credit. They had hopes and dreams and, though I loved them very much, they had given up and reconciled themselves to be downtrodden. They were dear souls, but they gave up.

I think I read this on a place mat in a truck-stop diner, "It's not how many times you get knocked down that matters, it's how many times you get back up."

We didn't just decide to commit to *Clients First*, then tell the staff about it and ride off into the sunset holding hands. We fought for *Clients First*. We struggled. We never gave up.

One of the hardest things any business does is to hire and train good help. Often, the temptation when presented with a poor performer is to put up with the situation rather than go to all the trouble of finding a replacement. Here is where we have had to stand up for *Clients First*. We have a saying in our office that it is not the ones you let go who hurt you, it is the ones you keep who do all the damage. If someone on the team fails to put *Clients First*, we release them back into the workforce.

No, No, No

Let me tell you, there are a lot of business models out there that look mighty attractive, and they are all about making it easy on yourself and playing it smart and the heck with the clients. I know agents who fire difficult sellers and refuse to work with buyers who won't jump through a set of hoops designed to weed out the time wasters. I see businesses where management thinks it's all about them and their rules and their policies.

There is a restaurant in town that survives because the chef makes the best specialty dish to be found anywhere. I'm calling it a "specialty dish" to protect the restaurant's identity, because I don't want to hurt the owners. They make this dish like nobody else, and they should have made a fortune by now, but they are still in the same location doing the same business they have for years. Maybe that's all they want. I can't speak for them. They used to have several signs posted in the waiting area: No cell phones. No checks or credit cards. No shoes, no shirt, no service. No party will be seated until all are here. No smoking. No reservations. No takeout. No substitutions. No exceptions. Today, I noticed the no-cell-phones sign is gone, but I'm still afraid to make a call while waiting for my specialty dish. As I say, I can't speak for the owners of this restaurant. Their business is steady and unchanged. If they were to care at all about their customers, they would prosper beyond anyone's wildest dreams, but *Customers First* matters only if that is what they want—and apparently they do not.

Vigilance

When I see JoAnn persevere to the point of tears while some businesses seem to survive without putting their _Clients First_, when I find myself dealing with a difficulty for which the _Clients First_ option is not going to make things immediately easier—these are the times when it is important to keep the commitment. This is why it is important to speak the commitment. We must remind ourselves every day that putting _Clients First_ is the right thing to do, so that we may keep the commitment.

It is so easy to fall off the wagon. A bite of someone else's French fry today may lead to a 2,000-calorie breakfast the next morning. We forget, and we forget quickly. Once, I tripped and broke my finger when I fell. When I stood up, I looked down and saw that I had missed a two-inch step up in the sidewalk. Had it been a six-inch riser, I would have seen it coming and my finger wouldn't have ached like the devil. No, it is the little steps we miss. Falling away from a commitment isn't a giant blunder, it's a teeny-weeny mistake. For a moment, you let a client get to you and you think _I don't need this aggravation_, and the next day you are prejudging a walk-in and deciding whether you even want to bother with that person and his or her problems.

Clients First is a commitment you must keep every day. You must recommit every day.

Eventually, the habit sets in. Eventually, you become hardwired. The temptations go away. Keeping your commitment to putting _Clients First_ becomes easier. The benefits and rewards begin piling up. You begin to experience the thrills and satisfactions. Your life becomes easier. Your financial success grows. Keeping your commitment to putting _Clients First_ becomes automatic. Time passes, and you forget who you used to be and find yourself proud of the person you've become.

Now, if I can only say no to that cheeseburger.

Step 4

Get Yourself Out of the Way

Just ask our kids whether JoAnn and I are competitive, but make sure they don't have a mouthful of food when you do. We were driven, obsessive, compulsive, and just about every other adjective that might define successful people. Still, for all our passion to succeed, we were just as unsuccessful, just as stuck, as our lady in blue at the Mustang Library. At 50 years of age, we didn't have money. Our history was full of ups followed by downs. We had memories that were dear to us, but halfway through our lives we were still where we started.

Our egos controlled us instead of us controlling our egos. We were driven to win for the sake of winning. We wanted success, respect, adulation, and even the envy of our peers. We thought people would care if we achieved. We sought recognition. We were very much in our own way.

Redirection

It wasn't until *Clients First* that we channeled all that drive into taking care of our clients, and when we did, our clients took care of us.

This is your fourth step on the path. You must find a way to redirect your ego. It is your ego, your sense of self, so it will be up to you how you do it. But do it you must, for to be subject to your ambition is to be enslaved by a wicked master who will destroy you in the end. We can offer our experience and how it happened for us, but you will be the one to get yourself out of the way.

It's Your Elephant

But isn't it important to have a strong ego, a strong sense of yourself? Yes, as long as you are the one in charge. Think of it as owning an elephant. Elephants are raised with a small rope around their ankles tying them to a stake. A baby elephant can't pull this stake out of the ground, so the young elephant believes it cannot escape. As the elephant matures into a powerful creature, it continues to believe it cannot escape from this small tether. The elephant's handler uses this and other techniques to control the elephant. Now, with your elephant, you can lift great weights, clear debris, tow anything, and transport many people, provided you are in control. But the day you let your elephant run loose, everything in its path can be destroyed. Your commitment to *Clients First* can be the tether that keeps your elephant obedient. But it is a small rope and a big elephant, so you must have additional tricks up your sleeve, such as understanding self-importance.

Not on Their Radar

You are important to you. You must take care of yourself. You must eat right, fight bad habits, get some exercise. These things are up to you. If you don't take care of yourself, who will? Outside of your family and closest friends, you are not someone else's concern.

Others have their own concerns. They must worry about their blood sugar. They can or cannot quit smoking. They must strive to be good parents. They must be respectful children. They have their own hopes and dreams. They have themselves to take care of, and you are just not on their radar.

There is an old saying: "When I was young, I thought everyone was thinking about me. As I grew older, I thought only a few people were thinking about me. Today, I realize nobody thinks about me at all."

Take care of yourself. Do a good job on you. Be the best you that you can be. Just don't think it matters to anyone else.

What's Best for Them

Now and then I have a client who will say something unusual about how hard we've worked and how we really deserve our commission. This is usually when we are *not* getting paid, because a deal is going south, or when the client has decided, after all our efforts, *not* to sell. The reason this strikes me as unusual is because I know most people are really only concerned with their self-interests. I never know whether such people are truly incarnations of Buddha or, more probably, just feel guilty. I tell them to forget about it, that all that is important to us is what is best for them, and I believe every word. Unearned commission should never be a client's concern. What matters to these people is what is best for them, and what matters to us is putting *Clients First*, which is whatever is best for them.

Also, every now and then I hear workers quoting the expense they've gone to in producing shoddy work, and I shake my head in disbelief. They say things like, "I've got 50 hours in this," or "I spent $1,000 on materials." The recipients of the poor job don't *care* about the cost of delivering bad results. They care about getting what they bargained for. Providers of goods and services have to get over themselves. People care about themselves and what is best for them. When executives in a company understand that, they will put their customers first and stop running self-serving commercials.

A Good Thing

Control your ego by knowing that you are important to you and that you are not important to others. This realization will keep your elephant well mannered and at times philosophical.

A healthy ego is a good thing. You want your elephant to be as big as your elephant can be. You want your elephant well fed, well groomed, and powerful. You want your elephant to be confident. You must believe in yourself. You must build your confidence. It is only with a strong sense of self that you can put your clients first and do a good job for them. Do you think your clients will be better served by some wilting wallflower, afraid to speak up for them, or by someone who will be strong for them because they are strong for themselves? This is where folks get things mixed up. They think that by serving others they must take a backseat. They think that blind obedience is good obedience. They think that clients want to always hear yes and to never hear no. Clients want a champion. They want a knight in shining armor. They want someone to protect and serve. And they want that person to be confident in whom they are.

Consequences

You must find a balance. You must get yourself out of the way. You must use your ego to put the *Clients First*. To fail in this, you will doom yourself to repeated failures and destroyed villages trampled in the wake of your rampaging ego. To better understand, let's look at some consequences of ego-driven efforts, the first of which is arrogance.

Arrogance is so stupid, but people fall into it every day. If you want to make villains more evil, make them arrogant. Everywhere we look the mighty are brought low and the masses cheer. If you want to be arrogant, you may as well paint a target on your backside to make it easier for your enemies, who grow in number hourly. Yet we slip into arrogance so easily.

Some people have a low opinion of this or that profession. They perceive car salespeople and politicians as less than honest. Lawyers and stockbrokers are fee churners. And doctors and Realtors are arrogant. Many act as though they are smarter than their patients or their clients, and a whole industry suffers the bad rap.

Arrogance is a compelling serpent whispering in our ear. We are beguiled by our small successes into thinking others are impressed. We begin to believe that our good fortune is because we are somehow better than the less fortunate. We begin to listen to our own boasting and begin to rejoice in it. Arrogance is a snowball rolling down a long slope with a whole town to be destroyed at the bottom. Yet we continue to be ensnared in the temporary good vibes of arrogance.

It can feel so good to put some people down. They deserve it. They did us wrong and now we get to pay them back. What better way than to rub their noses in our success? Envy, jealousy, and vengeance are avenues to arrogance and self-interest.

Not Popular

People just can't take themselves out of the equation. Many people think that building rapport is a matter of finding a common interest. Then they dominate the common interest discussion by talking about themselves. I used to do that in high school. Whatever came up, I would relate it to myself. Needless to say, I was not popular.

My cousin was popular. He pursued popularity with a drive any politician would envy. I used to smugly reject his efforts at popularity. I would tell myself it was beneath me to do the things he did just to be popular. I thought of myself as deep and sensitive. I thought he was shallow. He would laugh at jokes that were not funny. He would wave at cars when he didn't even know for sure who was in them. He would get everyone else to talk, and when he did speak, it was to say something nice about someone. He flattered, he encouraged, he cajoled. He was so popular that he probably remembers high school as the best time of his life.

I was wrong. I was the jerk. I was the arrogant one thinking I was too good to make the effort. I got better in time. In my 20s, I learned to stop interjecting stories about me. In my 30s, I learned to sell and ask qualifying questions. In my 40s, I swung back and forth between arrogance and embarrassment. Then JoAnn and I discovered *Clients First* and I got myself out of the way. I realized that for all the wonderful things JoAnn thought and felt about me, for all the mixed-up vanity I had inside, what mattered were the clients, not me.

Your Way

You must find your own way to control your ego. You must take care of yourself and be important to you. Just don't think you are important to people you don't know. They have their own problems to worry about. You must keep the commitment to putting *Clients First*, because that will keep you grounded. Build your confidence. Get good at what you do, and then get better. Confidence will make you decisive and strong for your clients. You must guard against arrogance and self-absorption. They will only tear down what you build. Put your *Clients First*.

When you've gotten yourself out of the way, you will be ready to set your monkey down. Get ready to set your monkey down!

Step 5

Set the Monkey Down

For all those years leading up to *Clients First*, I thought it was all up to me. Because JoAnn and I have a wonderful relationship and we share everything, she shared the burden with me, and it was all up to us. I am sure there were even times she thought it was all up to her. We carried the responsibility for our family and future like a monkey on our backs. But when we made our commitment to *Clients First*, we were able to set the monkey down.

At your fifth step, you, too, will become unburdened. You will stop pressing. You will find peace. You will find your way to get the monkey off your back.

Monkeys may be fabulous pets in real life. But in the dark world of emotions and responsibilities, monkeys are awful animals. They clutch and cling and weigh upon your back. They screech in your ear incessantly and pound at your head if they think they are being ignored. They must be fed and their messes cleaned up. And worst of all, they are nocturnal, becoming most active at night when you are alone with your thoughts, hoping for sleep, only to have your monkey clutching your shoulder and digging its nails into your skin.

Nobody Likes a Martyr

One of JoAnn's favorite stories about us took place when we were in our early 30s. She worked in a fine furniture store and I worked in a steel fabrication plant in Decatur, Illinois. Only two years before, we had been at a low ebb, broke and starting over. Our girls were 13, 12, and 7. We lived in a small rented house and had worked our way up from the bottom. I started out on the night shift, pressure-testing giant steel vessels, and was now working days and doing job estimating in the company office. JoAnn had risen from selling sofas to assisting the owner of the company in everything from purchasing to managing day-to-day operations.

We were finally getting ahead. We had a little money in the bank and were thinking of buying a new home. But to make that commitment required us to stay where we were, and neither of us wanted that. The girls missed us and we missed each other. The discussion of what to do went on for weeks. We wanted to move to Arizona and start over. I got pneumonia every winter. The furniture store was a family business, and JoAnn was not family. We both felt this huge responsibility weighing us down. Neither of us wanted to make a decision that for us would be life changing. We vacillated between the security of staying and the risk of change. Then, on a Sunday night with Monday morning looming, we found ourselves shouting in the kitchen. I finally voted to go and waited for an answer. She said, "Why does it always have to be me?"

I said, "You want me to decide without you?"

"No, but you're putting it all on me."

"Because I went first?"

She gave me a long litany of how she had to do this and had to do that. She felt the weight of the world on her shoulders.

Standing by the refrigerator, I took her in my arms and said, "JoAnn, nobody likes a martyr."

It was one of those special moments we get to share with those we love. In those few silly words, I had made the decision for us and relieved her of the burden. It could have just as easily been the other way around. She could have been the one to decide. She could have gotten the monkey off my back, but for the first time ever in our marriage, I made the decision for us. It was a gift I gave her.

We Make Our Own Monkeys

That is what happened to us that night when we decided to put *Clients First*. We made the decision and set the monkey down together.

For years, for our entire married lives, we had a series of monkeys on our backs. It seemed everything fell on us. We married young. Our parents didn't particularly approve. We had the girls and no help. We bore it all and did what we had to do, but we never had anywhere to look for support. All we had was each other, and collectively we carried our monkey.

Your situation may be different. You are unique. You may have had it much worse and had to overcome and endure terrible hardships. Conversely, you may have had what everyone else perceived as a silver-spoon life. Neither of these circumstances have anything to do with the monkeys we carry. Our monkeys are of our own making, and we all have them, no matter how good or challenging our circumstances.

If you have never felt the burden of life's responsibilities, you are fortunate. You have no monkey on your back. We did.

Clients First liberated us and set us free. When we decided to put *Clients First*, it was as though the monkey was suddenly gone. The success of our business was no longer on us. Our challenge was only to do the best for our clients. As long as we put our *Clients First*, the rest would take care of itself.

The Worry Chart

How do you set your monkey down? The obvious answer is stop feeding it. Animals are like that; they go where they are fed. What are you feeding your monkey? Worry is an addictive food. First you take on the miseries of the world and then you worry about it. It all depends on you, so you worry that you can't cope with it all.

I used to use fret and fear to feed my monkey. When nothing was wrong, I would look for trouble. Mark Twain said toward the end of his life, "I'm an old man and I've had many troubles, most of which never happened." Then one day, JoAnn gave me a worry chart. It was a cute little framed novelty she found in a gift shop. It said that 41 percent of our worries were things with little chance of happening, such as plane crashes and meteors striking the earth; 34 percent were things you probably cannot change, such as the unemployment rate, death, or taxes; 12 percent were in the hands of other people, and you couldn't control what they did; and 8 percent consisted of past mistakes you could not change. You can't turn back the clock. Aches and pains comprised 4 percent, which would either go away or get worse, in which case you could worry about that then. And about 1 percent of the things you worry about you just might have the power to fix.

Clients First takes away the worry, because whether you succeed or fail is no longer about you. You may succeed or fail for your clients, but all that matters is that you did your best for them. There is no monkey. It is a win-win. The clients put their faith in you, and you put your faith in doing your best for them.

Detachment

Another way to express this was articulated by a gentleman who may never have realized what a profound thing he was saying. He was talking about being philosophical when cold-calling strangers for business. He was advising his audience on how to cope with rejection. When JoAnn and I heard this, we absorbed it differently. We've never made cold calls and don't plan to, but his words struck a chord. He said, "The more detached you are from the outcome, the more attached the outcome becomes to you."

The more you say it, the more it hits you. In Las Vegas, they say *scared money never wins*. In boardrooms, they say *you can't get to yes unless you are prepared to accept no*. The more detached you are, the better your chance for success. Clients hire us because they are too close to the result. They are emotional. They are involved. They hire us for the detachment. That's one of the services we provide. That is not to say we don't care for our clients. We do. Sometimes I think we care more than our client does. But detachment allows us to care without jeopardizing the potential result. The monkey is off our back, because we are putting our clients first, and that is the best thing we can do.

You Can Change

Unlike much of our *Clients First* experience, this was not instantaneous. I believe a better description of what happened to us would be that our monkey stopped chattering one day and then one night just wandered off. We were so into *Clients First* that we hardly noticed. Then one day we looked at each other and remarked that *Clients First* sure made everything easier. It wasn't until years later that we used the monkey analogy to describe this phenomenon. We look back at who we were and shake our heads. They say people don't change, but don't you believe it. You *can* change. *Clients First* can change you. Some changes will be so sudden you won't see them coming; some will be so gradual you won't detect the movement. But change you can and change you will—and one day, you will wonder where your monkey went.

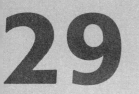

Step 6

Put Your Faith in Others

JoAnn and I used to be overwhelmed. We had so much to do and so little time. Our efforts were all about us and ours. We had no help and expected none. Then *Clients First* opened the door to serving others and, in turn, letting others help us. When we learned to put our faith in others, we found ourselves lifted as if by hundreds of unseen hands.

You, too, will be rewarded in something much greater than money when you reach step 6. You will find you are not alone when you open your eyes to the hopes, dreams, talents, and abilities of those around you. *Clients First* will open the window, and you will see a whole new world of people to make your life easier.

This step is a *twofer* (getting two things for the price of one). Putting your faith in others applies both to you serving others and to others serving you. This is a magical two-way street on which you will find yourself traveling back and forth every day without caring which direction you are going, because there are riches at both ends.

Forget about the Money

When you help other people, when you serve them, you should do so with a generosity of spirit and without regard to compensation. I'm not saying you should work for free. What I am suggesting is that you should separate the giving of the service from the paycheck. When you do this, when you give of yourself freely, you will find people return the service in the same way.

The goodness of serving others is not necessarily an unarguable given. In fact, most people question the concept on one or more levels. They ask what's in it for them, implying a distrust of a potential quid pro quo. People want to know the reward ahead of time, before they commit to doing something. If they do something for someone, who's to say they will be paid back?

Clients First changes that. When you commit to putting your *Clients First*, you commit to serving them. You commit to serving them without caring about the pay. JoAnn and I are often surprised at how rarely we think about an individual commission. Don't get me wrong. We look at our profit and loss statement monthly. Every day we track how much is coming in during the next month. We don't discount our services, and we don't try to sell a house without a listing agreement. But for any given negotiation, for any one client, the commission is the last thing we think of, if at all.

Years ago, we had our first multi-million-dollar sale. We represented the buyer, and Donna found a wonderful home for them in Paradise Valley. These clients had been referred to us by another client, and JoAnn was very caught up in doing a good job so that we reflected well on the client who had recommended us. We made the deal, escrow opened, and we moved on to the next client. After 30 days, we walked into the office and something was amiss. Everybody was in an especially good mood. Not that our office isn't generally cheerful, but true joy was in the air. It was like static. You have to understand that everyone in our office is an agent, and every time a transaction closes, each person receives a portion of the check. JoAnn and I even remarked to each other midmorning that it felt a little weird. It wasn't until just before lunch that someone remarked that the Paradise Valley sale was closing, and we realized the source of the excitement. Here we were, closing a sale for three times more than our previous high, and we had completely forgotten about the money.

Many Would Dispute This

This is the power of *Clients First*. You put your faith in serving others, and you just know that all will be well. Knowing and believing are what faith is about. You know the sun will come up tomorrow morning, and you believe it, and you have faith that it will. How about something a little less obvious? You know the government is watching the food industry, and you believe it, and you have faith that what you put on your table is safe to eat. Ah . . . not so fast. Not everyone agrees with that last statement. There are those who question the safety of our food supply. Maybe your next meal is okay and maybe it's not. When it comes to faith, you have to make up your own mind.

Now let's say that serving others is good, and you believe it, and you have faith. Unfortunately, many would dispute this as well. These skeptics ask, "What guarantees do you have that you'll get paid?" They have no faith in people. They can't comprehend putting *Clients First*. Of course, when their family sedan comes back from the car wash with water spots on the hood, just listen to them complain. They want to be put first. They want to be served. They just don't want to be the one to take the first step.

Quickly, Yet Slowly

Clients First is a leap of faith. You must take the plunge. You cannot decide to put your *Clients First* and then say, "After you."

You must go first. If you are waiting for the world to find its way to your doorstep, you can forget it. But if you step up and make that commitment to *Clients First* and do the things it demands of you, then the universe will beat a path to your foyer and make you a star. The more you elevate others, the greater your personal ceiling rises.

This change for us came quickly, yet slowly. JoAnn and I made the commitment that night, and we jumped in and devoted ourselves to putting *Clients First*, and things went well, and we got ourselves out of the way, and we put the monkey down, and everything became easy, and success flowed—but our faith grew much more cautiously. Every time we'd try and every time we'd win, it was like a little miracle, and our faith grew a little more. As time passed and we felt the benefits of people supporting us, we believed even more. Then one day we just knew. We knew the power of *Clients First*. We felt it deep down, like a fundamental tenet. *Clients First* was real.

Miracles

It doesn't matter what your religious affiliation is, or even whether you have one, I am here to tell you that faith and miracles do happen. I don't know if it's a physical law of vibrational energy or a new-age touchy-feely thing, but it is real, and when it happens, the hair on the back of your neck stands up and you take notice.

A short time after we experienced our *Clients First* moment, we listed a home on Delcoa Avenue, which our client had remodeled extensively, doing most of the work himself. It sold at the first open house to a couple moving from south Scottsdale, and they hired us to sell their home as well, which we did only a week later. I'll never forget this couple, whom we represented both as buyer and seller. Although they were middle-aged, they were almost childlike in their understanding of the process. He had a good job and she was a stay-at-home mother, and they emanated a goodness that can only be described as "sweet."

We commenced escrow on both homes and sat down with them to discuss the inspection report on the Delcoa house, the one they were purchasing. It was awful. It was typical do-it-yourself workmanship, and the list of deficiencies was long. We recommended that they ask for extensive repairs, and I'll never forget what she said: "No, we can fix these later. I know that our house will need a lot of things, too, but if we don't ask these folks to fix anything, our buyer won't either."

Sure enough, the inspection report on their south Scottsdale home came in a few days later, and it was even worse than that of the Delcoa property. Imagine our surprise when the agent representing that buyer sent us an addendum accepting the home with no repairs.

If you hear the theme music to *The Twilight Zone*, you are not alone, but we have been in this business long enough to tell you these little miracles occur all the time, and when they do, it is because someone took a leap of faith.

Faith is a powerful engine, and you can have it for free. All it takes is a little belief, and miracles drop from the sky like raindrops in April.

Take a Chance

You will have your own journey of faith. If you are a person who already believes in the goodness of humankind, your trip may be short and sweet. If you are a diehard pessimist, then you must find that initial point of beginning and say, "*I think I can, I think I can.*" Wherever you are between these two extremes, you will need to begin. Put your faith in the service of others.

"But how can I do this? What if I don't get paid? What if I get cheated?" Do you hear yourself? Do you want to go through life never trusting in anybody or anything? Sometimes you have to take a chance. What is the risk? Have you gotten the short end of the stick before? Did your caution and lack of faith protect you? If your answer is no, then what do you have to lose? Accept that sometimes you're going to be left holding the bag, and there is nothing you can do about it. But by putting your faith in others, you open yourself up to winning all those other times when your previous reticence might have caused you to fail. It is better to try than to have never made the effort. This is a crossroads. You are at the next step. Either you follow the arrows or you may as well go home.

Start with the next customer who crosses your path. Start with your boss, who is a client for your services. Start with an employee, because you are giving that person an opportunity. Look at that client and think how you can serve. What can you do for this person? Don't think about what you'll get in return. Just put your faith in the service of this fellow human being. Then go on to the next client and the next. Let the power of serving others be unleashed. In time, you will have a little faith, then you will believe, and ultimately you will know. This is what *Clients First* can do for you.

Letting Go

The other side of putting your faith in the service of others is delegation or leverage. The fact is, there is only so much we can do by ourselves. Given that we all have the same 60 minutes in each hour and the same 24 hours in each day, then how do we account for some people getting so much done and others so little? The answer is that they buy time.

They do this by delegating tasks to others, or they leverage themselves by asking others to duplicate their efforts entirely, thereby multiplying their accomplishments. The success of this time purchase relies on putting your faith in the service of others. If you don't believe another person can do a given task or do what you do, then your efforts at getting more done are doomed.

I was the worst at delegation. I was a proponent of the old phrase, "If you want something done right, do it yourself." I couldn't let go, and, as a result, I was limited in what I could accomplish. JoAnn was better than me, but there were things she couldn't let go of. We did everything and almost ran ourselves into the ground. After three years in the business, we were exhausted. Today, we do three times the work with one-third the effort. We put our faith in our team and they take care of us.

I'll never forget when we decided to train our daughter Kelly to go on listing appointments. This seemed to be the last thing we couldn't let go of. In eight years, we estimated that we had gone to more than 10,000 appointments. We worried that people expected to see us at the door. What would Kelly do? How could Kelly do what we did? We calculated that our business might decline by 50 percent, but we accepted that possibility because we were torn between working *in* our business and working *on* our business. We had to take a leap of faith.

How did it work out? It is embarrassing to say, but Kelly does every bit as well as we ever did. Clients love her. She puts them first, and our business never dropped a dime. This is the power of putting your faith in the service of others.

A Twofer

You will find yourself carried by those around you. You will have more time because you will have help. You will have more business, because those clients you put first will work to help you. No matter where you are, whether you are the company CEO, work on the line in a factory, wait on customers, or track accounts receivable, putting your faith in others will come back to you a hundredfold.

Remember, this is a twofer. Faith can birth miracles.

Step 7

Trust the Truth

Looking back on the past dozen years since we changed, since *Clients First* changed us, I am at a loss to explain our honesty now compared to then. We felt honest back then. If someone were to question our honesty, our reaction would have been the same as yours. "Of course we are honest. How can you even ask?" But today, as difficult as it might be to explain, I know there is a difference. We are not the same. Today, we put our *Clients First*. Today, we trust the truth.

Trust is a powerful concept. That we can place our faith in another human being, in an idea, or even in things is a wonderful assurance. We put our trust in our parents, our life partner, and our children. We trust our government, our principles, and our ideals. We trust our tools to get the job done, and we trust a McDonald's in Spokane to deliver the same Big Mac as a McDonald's in Miami Beach. It is good to trust.

Trust brings us joy. Trust makes us feel safe. We want to trust. We need to trust our environment and the people around us.

But what happens when a trust is broken? The betrayal by another is a pain so great it seems impossible to bear. When we feel let down by our institutions, or even our favorite tire store, our disappointment can be overwhelming. This hurtful potential makes us cautious, and in the end our trust is reduced to a question: Dare we trust?

When it comes to the truth I urge you to not only trust the truth, but to trust the truth *daringly*. We must put aside caution. We must not ask what the consequences are. Everything we do has an impact, but not trusting the truth is always more expensive than trusting the truth.

Better for It

How many times do we hear that the greater crime is not a momentary lapse of good judgment, but rather in the cover-up that follows? Watergate, a simple burglary, brought down an American president who thought he could cover it up. Had Richard Nixon taken responsibility for the poor selection and even poorer management of some of his closest advisers, had he trusted the truth and cleaned house, the American people might have reelected him. Even if they had not, Nixon's disgrace would have been mitigated and we would have been better for it.

We are human beings, and with that fact comes the realization that we are not perfect. We make mistakes. Were it not for our mistakes, we would not learn from our life experiences. Yes, mistakes have consequences. Accept them and move on. Trust the truth and it will bring you joy and peace.

This is your next step on the path to *Clients First*. With this step, you will grasp and hold the key of honesty. This key alone will change everything and everybody around you, and yet it is a mystery to explain how. How do you achieve honesty? If you feel honest now, how do you know you aren't already there? Before you began this book, you probably felt that you were putting your *Clients First*. How do you feel now? If you don't feel a difference, even if you cannot yet explain it, then you either already do put your *Clients First* or you need not try. If you haven't made the commitment to put your *Clients First*, if you cannot see yourself as you were and as you want to be, then you need to first ask whether you are being honest with yourself.

JoAnn and I know we were different before *Clients First*. Today we trust the truth and can look in the mirror and say that our honesty then was not the same as our honesty now. We were not always sure we could trust the truth. We feared consequences. We feared not being in control. We tried to make things happen according to plan. We held back. We sought to manipulate. We did so with the best of intentions, but as we look back, it was not the same then.

We Failed

You want proof? Has all this so far been a nice story and a feel-good premise? Then I will come clean and confess. During the REO boom, we screwed up royally. For all our competence, we messed up big-time. It is our job to protect our bank clients and take care of their property while it is assigned to us. This includes making sure the bank has accurate information upon which to make its decisions. We are to know all, see all, and be all for our clients. Remember, this is a one-strike business. Well, we failed.

We missed a homeowners' association assessment, and two days prior to closing, an unexpected $3,800 expense was to appear on the proposed closing statement. This was a major strike one. Worse yet, this was our biggest client. Safe to say, losing this bank could mean a major restructuring of our business. To top it all off, the asset manager assigned to the property (and therefore the person to whom we answered) was by reputation the oldest of old-timers with the bank and the toughest on agents. We knew this from other agents who spoke of being cut off for the smallest infraction of the rules.

When JoAnn learned of the error it was 10:00 AM, and instead of just picking up the phone, she froze. What should we do? How could we explain? It was a team member who screwed up, but it was still our fault. She could offer to pay the expense, but even so, the damage was there. Banks have procedures and rules. The crime had been committed, and paying the fine didn't change the record. JoAnn knew she had to call, but she did something she never does: She waited. The waiting only made it worse. She anguished. JoAnn knew this asset manager well and had handled previous properties for the woman. JoAnn knew she was in California, an hour behind us, and that she worked late. JoAnn waited the whole day, made herself sick, and didn't know what to do.

At seven o'clock, we went home. JoAnn sat at our kitchen booth, cell phone in hand, and asked me what to do. I told her we had only one choice, that we were even writing a book on it. We had to tell the straight truth, offer to make good the expense, and accept the consequences. She tapped in the numbers.

The asset manager answered. She listened as JoAnn related the error, offered to pay, and accepted responsibility. A long pause ensued. Finally, the woman said she had managed the sale of more than 1,000 bank assets and had dealt with at least half that many agents. In all that time, she said she never had an agent do what JoAnn just did. She said there were hundreds of explanations JoAnn could have offered, and she had probably heard them all, but never had an agent been so plainly honest with her. She said to add the homeowners' association charge to the closing statement and send it in the morning. When JoAnn repeated that we felt responsible and wanted to pay the fee, this woman said no, she would not allow it. When JoAnn finally asked whether we would lose the bank over this, she was told that she not only would not lose the bank, but that this woman would be her champion should the opportunity ever arise.

JoAnn hung up and wept. I held her, and we realized that we were once again saved by the miracle that is *Clients First*.

Embrace the Truth

Today we enjoy a wonderful calm. We don't worry about what we said last week, last month, or even this morning. Whatever we do, we trust in the truth, and that makes our path easy. Do we suffer consequences? Of course we do, but they are immediate, so we deal with them and move on. If you get nothing else here, understand this: The consequences of trusting the truth are always minuscule compared to the consequences of not trusting the truth.

How do you achieve *Clients First* honesty? Trust the truth. How do you take this chance? There is a risk, after all. You don't want to put your faith in something that will let you down. You don't want the pain. Do you fear the truth? There are those who do. Don't be one of them. Embrace the truth as if it were your lover. The truth will never betray you. Trust the truth and you will have a companion who will never disappoint you.

Begin today, right now. Think about your relationship with the truth. Ask yourself tough questions. Achieve honesty with yourself and then go on to others. This is your next step on the path to *Clients First*.

Start with the next person you see. See him or her as a person just like you. Do people want the truth any less than you? They want to trust. They need to trust. Be honest. Give them what they need. Give them the truth and you will be joined together in a bond that never betrays.

The Truth of *Clients First*

Your clients will know when you've changed. Ours did. They will feel your honesty on an unseen plane. Ours did. And they will trust you as never before, because they will know you are putting them first.

As you grab onto this powerful rocket, you will be transported beyond the gravity of fear and consequences. You will walk free among the stars, and your clients will look up to you and say, *"There is an honest person. There is someone I can trust to take care of me. There is someone who will tell me the truth. There is someone who puts me first."*

Then they will bring their neighbors and friends and family. They will recommend you and advocate for you and want you to succeed. And when you take care of those they bring to your care, it will reflect well upon their recommendation, and they will be proud and will seek to do it again and again.

This is the truth of *Clients First*. This is the truth you can trust.

31

Step 8

Let the Work Be the Reward

O n JoAnn's desk are a number of little reminders and memories precious to her. One that she has had for a long time is a saying credited to Confucius: "Love what you do and you will never work another day in your life."

A million years ago, when we were very young and our girls were all in elementary school, we found ourselves in a new part of town with enough money for the first month's rent on a little house and about a week's worth of groceries. We didn't have a car. My most pressing concern was health insurance for our family of five, so when I looked in the newspaper for a job, I needed one within walking distance and with benefits from day one. There it was. The local hospital needed housekeeping help. I applied and started the next evening.

Insanity

I was placed with another young man named Mike for training, and he showed me where the supply closets were and how the system worked. First thing, we reported to the shift manager and got a job slip. The tasks ranged from waxing halls to completely sanitizing patients' rooms after they went home. Although he had been there four years, Mike was not happy with the work, and he rushed through every task. Consequently, his work was borderline substandard, and on the third night of my employment, we even had to redo a hallway. I could never figure out why Mike did this. He would rush through a job only to go back down to the manager's office to get another one. It was like the definition of insanity. Mike kept doing the same things and expecting a different result.

On my fourth night, I was assigned my own slip, and I went to a vacated room to wash the ceiling, scrub the walls, mop the floor, and wipe every surface clean. I took my time, putting myself into doing the best job I could. I probably took twice as long as Mike would have, but that room was clean when I finished. And so it went for about six weeks. Then one evening the shift manager called me into her office and told me I was going to go on the day shift. She added that in all her 32 years with the hospital she had never had anyone do such a good job.

I worked at the hospital for another two months before I found a union job at twice the wages, but I look back with pride on the job I did there. I didn't love cleaning messes found only in a hospital at midnight. It wasn't a career choice. But, unlike Mike, I figured I had to be there anyway, so I invested myself in the work and did a good job. Yes, I took the job to feed and protect my family, but more precious than the money and the work were the words of that shift manager. They were all the reward I needed.

Choice, No Choice

Confucius didn't say "do what you love," although given the choice, you should choose something you like to do. Instead, that wise man said you should "love what you do." We don't always have a choice. But we can choose how we deal with what we have to do. Choose pride in your work.

The second key to *Clients First*, competence and getting good at what you do, comes from letting the work be the reward. *Clients First* keeps you focused on the work. With *Clients First*, you forget about the money. You forget about the time. You don't care about the perks. You care about doing the job and doing the job right for your client. In real estate, JoAnn and I found a vocation we loved. *Clients First* made the work itself rewarding.

Step number eight on the path to *Clients First* may change your life. *Clients First* makes you question whether you love what you do. Unless you are willing to be the best at what you do, you aren't putting your *Clients First*, and if you go through your life doing something in which you cannot find enjoyment, you will be miserable. *Clients First* requires that you choose to let the work be the reward.

Greener Pastures

"What I'd really like to do is to direct," says the actor. "I'm just doing home inspections until drywall demand comes back," says the workman. "I'm just driving a cab until I finish night school for accounting," says the woman behind the wheel. Everywhere I look, people are looking to better themselves or hoping to find greener grass just beyond the fence. Some do a good job in their current endeavors and some don't. The ones doing a good job now will probably go on to do well in the future. The ones who don't do a good job currently truly believe that going to that next big thing is going to change how they feel about what they do—and that when that happens, they will somehow be transformed and become very good at whatever it is, because they will finally be doing what they love. Don't bet your life savings on it. These hopefuls will more likely find fault with their newly realized dream and begin talking about what they really want to do all over again.

Until they love what they do now, they will never love what they do when they land that dream job. *Clients First* is not something you will practice only when you get to management or become CEO. Clients First is something you do today, whether you are selling a pair of socks, installing brake pads while working on an assembly line, or cleaning a hospital room. Love what you do. Put yourself into doing the best job you can, no matter what it is. Your clients will appreciate your pride and feel elevated that you cared to do a good job for them. When you make them feel that you put them first, they will never leave you.

A Special Shine

I have seen this pride in the work of others, and some people show the greatest pride in the most menial tasks. I once had my shoes shined at the St. Louis airport. I had flown in for a very important appointment, and my shoes looked scuffed, so I stopped at this man's one-chair stand, climbed up, and put my foot on the worn metal rest. He was very old and slightly built. He applied the polish with browned fingers that matched my shoes. He talked to himself as he worked, mentioning, for example, how one of my heels was scratched and that he had a special concoction to fix it. As he stropped the shine cloth repeatedly over my toes, he stopped and peered into the finish to see if he could see his reflection.

I asked him about his family, and he said he had three sons, all professionals, and a daughter still in college. She wanted to be an astronaut. Another customer came along, and the old man acknowledged him with a nod and a "Be right with you," but he didn't rush to finish my shoes. He concentrated on the job in front of him and gave me the best shine I've ever had.

The rest of that day, and for several days after, I thought about that noble gentleman every time I looked at my gleaming shoes. I wondered what dreams he may have had as a young man. I wondered at what those four children might have made of themselves on the streets of St. Louis had it not been for his example. He loved what he did, and it showed. He made me feel special, and though I've never returned to that particular spot, I've mentioned to several fellow travelers that the St. Louis airport was a great place for a shoe shine.

Pride

For all of the wonderful stories of craft and competence, I see hundreds of examples of incompetence. One of the local supermarkets employs a special-needs young man as a bagger, and it is a pleasure to watch him decide which items should go in first so as to not crush the bread or crack the eggs. At another market where we shop, JoAnn has to supervise the bagging for fear we'll have our fruit bruised before we get to the car. On one occasion, JoAnn had to leave the store to take a phone call, and I watched a young girl load four of our bags without once looking down, because she was busy discussing her boyfriend with the cashier. I don't believe she will ever be happy with any job, and if she marries her boyfriend, he should probably learn to cook and clean house, because she'll be busy texting her friends about how she'd rather be doing something else.

Take pride in your work. Do your best. Get better. Take classes, go to seminars, and attend conventions. Be competent for your clients. Do what you love, but more important, love what you do. The work can be the reward, and when you let that happen, the work can make you proud.

Don't Wait

You can be an example to others. When you put your *Clients First* by doing a great job, you elevate your client, yourself, and everyone around you.

And if you just can't take it anymore, quit. Make a change. Don't do anything just for the money. Until you can love what you do, you will be miserable and will make everyone around you miserable. If you do a poor job, you will drive clients away. A sloppy result will only destroy any opportunity you might have, and in the end you will be broke and a disappointment to yourself and others. Don't wait until the bitter end. Take charge of your destiny and find what you love. Do it and love what you do. You will never work another day in your life.

Step 9

Learn to Like People

A real estate trainer I know speaks to large audiences of agents, some of whom are 30-year veterans and some of whom are brand new. He often uses this icebreaker to bridge the gap: He asks everyone to raise their hands, then he tells the people who have been in the business a long time to put their hands down. Then he asks those with less experience to drop their hands, and so on, until he gets down to the newest, freshest agent, who, for some unexplainable reason, always seems to be about 25 and female. Maybe the guys are just chicken. Anyway, he then asks why she has entered the real estate profession, coaxing out of her that she just loves houses and she just loves people. To this, he will shake his head slowly, with great gravity, and say, "Give it six months and you'll hate 'em both." The comic relief is tangible. The the audience roars, because the reality of real estate is that our profession is just as much, if not more, about people than the product we sell. Some, and JoAnn is among them, would argue that it is *all* about people, and I tend to agree.

It really doesn't matter whether your business is importing cowhides from Argentina for leather jackets that people wear or building nuclear power plant control panels so that people will have electricity. All business is about people, and if you are to be successful in business, you must care about the people you ultimately serve.

Far to Go

The first half of my life I had a few friends, dealt with family, and got lucky enough to find JoAnn. I cried at movies and gave to a few charities when asked. I thought of myself as socially adjusted. By comparison, JoAnn has always been more social than I am, but she's had her own challenges, one of which is putting up with me. We were normal. _Clients First_ changed us. Suddenly, we had a reason to care about others. Our clients looked to us, and if we were to do whatever it took to keep them, we had to care. As much as we thought of ourselves as nice people, _Clients First_ made us see how far we had to go. Silly as it sounds, we had to learn to like people.

You may already think of yourself as a people person, or you may have a long way to go, but when you arrive at step 9, you will learn the joy of people. _Clients First_ will open you to seeing people in a new way. You will want to know their stories.

People are fascinating. Ask whether someone has brothers and sisters, and you may open up a series of sibling rivalry tales or, conversely, learn about the solitude of being an only child. Ask people what they were doing on 9/11, and you may be surprised at how connected our world is. Everyone has a story to tell. You need only ask a few questions to cue the storyteller.

Learning Their Story

One of my favorite periods in our real estate career was at the very beginning, when we had no skills, no contacts, and I had a lot of fear. I decided to go out our front gate and knock on doors. We mapped out the square mile around our house, and it consisted of 1,000 homes. Every day I knocked on 30 to 40 doors, hoping to visit each occupant once a month. I had a business card that said REAL ESTATE on it, but knowing so little about the business and the market, I steered clear of real estate and asked questions of the folks who would talk to me. I asked how long they had lived here and where they were from. One thing would lead to another, and I would learn their story. Sometimes I learned embarrassingly too much about the neighbors, but I've never been one to gossip, so I didn't pass it on.

This was before our *Clients First* experience, so I would have to credit my fear of saying something stupid about real estate for my newfound interest in people, but it was a profound experience in my life. For the first time, I was learning to like people. At the end of the third month, JoAnn and I had too many clients for me to keep up the door knocking routine, and I had to let it go. At the time, I thought this exercise was unproductive in obtaining business, but as I look back, I realize that we've sold more than a third of those homes in the past 12 years. We still knock on doors—only now we have an appointment.

Don't Prejudge

Get to know the people in your business. Ask about their families. Feel their joys. Share their pains. Listen to their stories. As you do so, you will learn to like people, and when you like them, you will find it natural to put them first as clients.

What about the unlikable people in this world? What about the villains and sociopaths? What about the ornery ones who just have bad attitudes? You might be surprised when you ask them a few personal questions. You might learn that underneath that gruff exterior is a person you can like. I'm not saying there is goodness in all people, but I am saying we discard a lot of goodness for fear of asking or by prejudging.

Liking People

When JoAnn and I made the commitment to put our *Clients First*, we didn't restrict that commitment to the clients we liked, we committed to liking all our clients. You can't make clients feel special while remaining aloof and reserved. You can't put *Clients First* while being a stranger to them and having them be strangers to you. *Clients*

First is based on honesty, competence, and care. How can you care about someone you keep at arm's length? Caring is about engaging and knowing clients. Practice getting to know your clients. Learn to like people.

We have a sign in our office that says, "Clients don't care about how much you know until they know how much you care." Every time I read that poster I want to add the words "about them" to the end. Another way to put it is this: People don't want to do business with you until they want to do business with *you*. They want to do business with people they like, and they like people who like them.

Is it easy to like people? For some, it comes naturally. These are like JoAnn and the twentysomething newbies who raise their hand so the speaker can tell a joke and make a point. For others, it is a process taken on knowingly and not without struggle. These are like me, and I understand your reluctance. People can be a source of pain, ridicule, or embarrassment. But if you get out there and engage, begin showing an interest, and start asking friendly questions, you will find that everyone is just like you—filled with trepidations and worries, hopes and dreams. Learn their stories and you will learn to like people.

Open Up

Clients First has blessed JoAnn and me. The decision to take what comes in stride and concentrate on just taking care of the client has given us success we would never have otherwise achieved. Our resolve to keep the client, no matter the consequences, has not only allowed us to keep the client but brought us more clients. *Clients First* made it all so easy. I think of how we struggled before, and I see others struggling today, and I am grateful to have discovered *Clients First*. But *Clients First* has done so much more for me. It has opened me up to people.

Today, I want to stand up and say, "I love houses and I love people, and every six months I love them even more."

Step 10

Turn It Around

Frank Sinatra sings "My Way" and my heart swells. I heard General Norman Schwarzkopf speak on leading with a clear vision, and I was so impressed. We all admire the undaunted hero whose mind is made up and can't be changed. For most of my life, I was stubborn and closed-minded and took refuge in the belief that my point of view was the only one that mattered. Then one night, in struggling with a real estate deal, I had to turn it around and understand that the Smiths needed to hold out for more money and that the Browns, though they loved the house, could not afford it. JoAnn and I have been turning it around ever since.

This tenth step opens you up to how others see things, and to how they see you. By turning your viewpoint around to their viewpoint, you become perceptive. *Clients First* gives you new eyes and 20/20 vision.

Perspective

Do you realize that your right eye doesn't see the same thing your left eye sees? Try a little experiment. Hold your right hand about six inches in front of your face. Now close your left eye and look at your hand and what you see beyond it. Then close your right eye and look with your left eye. You are seeing two different scenes. This is because your right eye is seeing your hand and what is around it from the right side of your head and your left eye's viewpoint is from the left side. It is because we see from these two different points that we can judge depth and distance. People with the use of only one eye complain that they cannot tell how far away things are. They have trouble driving a car or even grabbing a doorknob. They lack perspective.

Before *Clients First*, we lacked perspective. JoAnn and I looked at the world through our eyes and our eyes only. We had gone through our growing-up years, a time when we knew everything and prided ourselves on being able to argue any side of any issue. This was, however, only a sophomoric attempt at open-mindedness, which, of course, we also knew all about. As we got older, our minds narrowed as our waists grew broader. When we found ourselves that night committing to taking care of the client, no matter how it served or didn't serve us, we realized we had to change our perspective.

To put *Clients First*, we had to see the world through their eyes. We had to care about getting them what they wanted. We had to turn it around.

Occasionally, when I'm being really stupid, JoAnn will quote to me a Robert Burns line she learned as a child. "And would some Power the small gift give us, to see ourselves as others see us." Wham, that puts me in my place. She also tells me that if I'm looking to blame someone, I should start with a mirror. As you can see, she is very supportive. But without JoAnn I would truly be lost. She saves me from myself. She grounds me. She tells me to turn it around.

A Made-Up Mind

I have this vendor—we'll call him Jim—who came to me for help one day. Jim has a home-cleaning business and wanted to expand it. Our real estate marketing is highly visible, so he wanted advice on what to advertise. I said I would help, and I worked on it off and on for about a month before we met again. Because I knew this fellow did good work and I knew what was important to our clients when we recommended him, I had put together a marketing plan based on those perceptions. I had a logo sketched and a font style picked out.

I had designed a flyer that related to his potential customers describing the benefits he offered.

When we met, Jim kept shaking his head. He had this affinity for a particular professional sports team and wanted his advertising theme to be based on that organization's branding. He had metaphors about beating the dirt and shutting out the tough stains. His mind was made up, and he only wanted me to agree with him and possibly make his idea better. He had given no thought to his customers or what they wanted or how they saw him and his service. He could not turn it around.

Jim runs his business like so many do. He offers what he offers, and if it's not what you want, then you can go somewhere else. He is lucky he does what he does so well, because that alone allows him to eke out a living. His desire to get more business, however, has never been realized, because he fails to see anyone's vision but his own. He doesn't see that not all of his potential clients are sports fans and, for that matter, that he might actually be alienating the ones who root for another team.

What Clients Want

Many businesses start out by seeing what their clients want. Entrepreneurs know that they must find a need and fill it. Then something happens. Companies become larger, and they reinvest that initial success in themselves, and they gradually lose track of their customers. Their businesses become all about them. Detroit automakers did this and gave away half their business to companies who listened to what people wanted. Airlines were so sure that people wanted assigned seats and slow connections that Southwest Airlines has profited from easy boarding and short hops. Honda hasn't forgotten that its customers want economy and a car that keeps going for 100,000 miles or more. BMW hasn't forgotten that its drivers want precision performance. While department store names piled up in the dustbin of history for their refusal to change their product mix, Sam Walton hooked his cash registers up to his warehouses to measure client preferences, and he never forgot that Walmart customers wanted the good things in life for less.

When Henry Ford invented the assembly line and produced his Model T, he was quoted as saying that folks could have any color they wanted . . . as long as it was black. It was a good joke and probably wouldn't work today, but what he did do was fill a need for affordable transportation, which transformed this nation. Ford never forgot his customers. They wanted a dependable, low-price vehicle that they could repair themselves, and for the better part of a century, Ford gave them just that.

It might be noteworthy to point out that when the Ford Company built a car to honor Henry's son, executives gave little thought to the potential customer. The Edsel was all about what *they* wanted, and sales were so anemic that the production line shut down in three years.

What the Client Sees

You can always benefit from seeing your business from your clients' point of view rather than your own. In fact, when you think about it, your company is not what you perceive it to be at all. Your company is only what your customers see. If your customers see your company as a self-serving enterprise that has a my-way-or-the-highway attitude, then your company will be seen as putting them last, and they will go elsewhere. If your customers see your company as putting *Clients First*, then those customers will be loyal and bring their friends.

As we were growing our business, and shortly after that moment when we committed to putting *Clients First*, I sat down to create a flyer. I needed a tagline, so I thought about our potential sellers and what they wanted. Yes, they wanted to find a good agent, and I could write something about how good our service was. Yes, they wanted top dollar (who doesn't?), and I could say something about how much harder we work and how aggressively we would negotiate for them. But in the end, I realized that all they wanted was to sell their property. They didn't really care who did it for them, and they would be the ones to ultimately say yes or no to the amount offered. What they wanted was the *result*, and I focused on that.

In Our Clients' Shoes

As soon as we made any deal, the first thing we did was go out and hang a SOLD sign. This became the symbol of the homeowner's success. It told the neighbors they had won. It kept the buyer committed, and it made our phone ring with new sellers. I wrote some long paragraph about how clients wanted to get their house sold and that we could achieve that result for them, and it was awful. It was wordy and flowery and full of ego. So I cut and cut and cut some more. When I finished I had, "When you want a sold sign . . ." We have used this line ever since. I've had clients repeat it back. I had one client who made a musical jingle out of it. We often have sellers ask the minute we make a deal, "When do we get our sold sign?" These six words have kept us in our sellers' shoes. They keep us focused. Our sellers may want many things—advertising, open houses, Realtor tours, top dollar—but at the end of the day, they want a sold sign.

Put yourself in your clients' place. See things from their eyes. Turn it around and improve your perception. If you are to put *Clients First*, you must care about what they want, and the best vantage point for what they want is from their viewpoint. Turn things around to see how your clients see you and your business. It will keep you true to their needs. It will bring you lasting success.

Step 11

Give to Get

I always knew the price of everything, and I always wanted to get a good deal. Early in our marriage, JoAnn clipped coupons so we could buy groceries at a savings. I had both hourly jobs and salaried positions, and I always measured what I was getting for my time. Then I was confronted with something that had no price: *Clients First*. It can't be quantified or measured. You can't just give a certain amount of honesty, competence, and care. With *Clients First*, I discovered something priceless, yet immeasurable in its reward.

The final step on the path to *Clients First* is realizing that the more you give, the more you get. With *Clients First*, you look for ways to give more, and the more you give, the more health, wealth, and happiness is returned to you.

You Can't Give It Away

There is a riddle that asks, "What can you give away and still have?" Sounds tough, doesn't it? I mean, it makes no sense. If you give something away, you don't have it anymore. Actually, I've heard this one with several different answers once you know the twist. My favorite is—a *smile*. Other answers are *love*, *kindness*, and even *a bad attitude* would probably work, but it's better to stick with positives.

The point is that we give away a lot of things besides money or possessions. And some of the things we give, we still have after the giving.

With *Clients First*, we give honesty, competence, and care. Do we have less of these things at the end of the day? No. Do we have more? Technically, the answer is no, but a case could be made for a cumulative positive effect. Giving these things over time does seem to create in the giver a larger capacity for the three keys. People who smile often tend to smile even more with time, just as people with frowns develop lines in their foreheads, thus making the next sad expression easier.

Giving Money

But what about real things, like money, houses, and cars? Since money can buy all these goodies, let's just *talk money*. How can you have money if you give it away? We aren't talking about a simple smile here. We are talking about real, hard-earned dollars. This is where the riddle breaks down. If you keep giving away money, you're going to go broke.

Let me tell you about the biggest giveaway we ever had, and you decide. Every year we send out Christmas ornaments to our clients. These are handmade from bread dough in the shape of a front door, and JoAnn designs a new one each year. One year, the ladies who produce these treasures were unable to work, and we needed an alternative. Our granddaughter suggested we help Habitat for Humanity build a house and make the donation in the name of "the Clients of Those Callaways." This sounds innocent enough, but one thing led to another, and we ended up donating $70,000 for a whole house. On the day we cut the check, I had to move some money around, which included not paying the full amount on our Visa account and transferring money from our personal savings. I remember telling myself over and over that this was a good thing to do. I'm sure there were sweat stains on the check where I signed.

We were apprehensive about how our clients would react. We sent our clients the usual cards, but instead of an ornament, we inserted a note saying that they had participated in the gift of a house to charity. We received a handful of sweet and supportive notes, but little else. I wrote it off to good karma and took several months to pay down our Visa account. Basically, I forgot about it; it was water under the bridge. We received a thank-you letter from the family who got the house, and JoAnn cried, and that was that.

Then, a few months later, as we were closing on a new home, the clients mentioned that they had seen the plaque on our wall and that it was one of their prime motivators in using us. Wow, I thought, a little payback. Another 20 or 30 deals and we'd be even. I gave it no more thought.

Over the years, we have had a number of similar incidents, all unsolicited. We never played on that single act of charity. But then one day we learned that one of the officers at a bank for which we sold foreclosed homes was very active with Habitat for Humanity. He told us he remembered what we did and that it was one of the reasons the bank went with us and stayed with us. This bank is local, and it ended up giving us all the business it had, which was enough to make the difference between our making it and not making it through our darkest market times. And here is the kicker. When the bank took ownership of a foreclosed mansion in Paradise Valley, our commission when we sold it was, you guessed, $70,000. Giving to get isn't the same as a financial transaction, where you give and get right then and there. There is no up-front agreement on what you will get for what you give. But rest assured, whatever you give will come back to you with interest. I like to think that this bank used us exclusively because we did a good job, which we did. But we may never have gotten that opportunity to demonstrate our skills had it not been for that one connection. It is impossible to quantify what that one gift has returned to us. We have no way of knowing all the stories and connections that act has consummated. We only know that the more we give, the more we get, and we look for ways to do more.

Immeasurable

Our local multiplex just celebrated its 20-year anniversary. JoAnn and I were there when it opened. It was the first night, and I don't remember the movie, but I remember that when we paid for the tickets they handed us two free passes for the next time we came. It was so neat that we came back only a couple days later to see our free movie. We weren't in real estate back then, so we actually had the time. Then, because we had seen a preview at the free movie, we returned again the following weekend, and when I bought the tickets received another pair of passes. It may as well have been narcotics. We were hooked. The theater kept this up for the first six months, and JoAnn and I never saw so many movies in our whole lives. They stopped giving the passes after that, but they do give free refills on the popcorn, and if you buy the souvenir cup, you pay only a dollar a drink for the whole year. Today, there are 26 multiplex theaters within 20 minutes of our home, and we still go back to the one that gave us free passes so long ago.

Clients First service is addictive like that. Your clients like special treatment. They get used to it, and eventually they can't imagine going anywhere else. You can't give too much. The more you serve your clients, the more they come back for more.

You will never get rich by being a miser. Success doesn't flow to those who hold back and measure what they are willing to invest. If you give little, you will have little given to you. Give all you have, and you will have all you want. You can't give it away.

35

Destination *Clients First*

I have friends who can drive to Las Vegas from Phoenix in three and a half hours. They can make it to Los Angeles without so much as a potty stop and flirt with the 75-mile-per-hour speed limit the whole way. JoAnn and I go about such trips in an entirely different way. When we go to Las Vegas, we have breakfast in Wickenburg, stop for apple pie and to feed the peacocks halfway to I-40, then take a break at the truck stop before Kingman, and then we decide whether to cross the Colorado River at Laughlin or go over Hoover Dam for the scenery. I'm sure we hold the record for the 200-mile drive to the quaint village of Greer in the White Mountains, at 12 hours and 37 minutes. We stopped three times in Fountain Hills alone, and it's only 15 miles from home. The reason these trips were so memorable is because we took our time and enjoyed the journey.

We stop at cute cafés and craft fairs. We sightsee at the scenic view pullouts; and, of course, we follow open house signs. It wasn't always like this, but somewhere along the way we learned that life isn't a destination. Life is a journey.

Staying in the Moment

I know folks who see Europe in a three-city, five-day whirlwind. When they get home, they have jet lag and can't remember the story that goes with each photo. We once drove from Milwaukee to Minneapolis, a 300-mile jaunt, over two nights and three days. I recall every moment.

The point here is not that we are slow travelers or that we are insensitive to the forward march of time. We live on deadlines. Everything we do is due now. We juggle, we delegate, and we hurry. But even in the rush of the day, we never think about the coming night. We stay in the moment and revel in the now. Life is the journey, not the destination.

The same is true of the path to *Clients First*. It is the path you will follow from now on. We have numbered the steps so you can stay on track, but *Clients First* is a wonderful journey full of twists and turns and sights to see. *Clients First* is a path you will never leave. Along the way, you will meet fabulous people on your *Clients First* journey. They will seem more fabulous because you will find them interesting and likable. You will want to serve them, and you will be rewarded beyond your imagination in return. Everything will become easier on your path to *Clients First*. You will set the monkey down, get yourself out of the way, and let the work be the reward. You won't want your journey to end.

So many people ask JoAnn and me, "What do you do to put *Clients First*?" They want a methodology. They want a checklist or an action plan. They want to have a meeting, delegate client care, and rush on with their lives, hurrying from destination to destination. They rush to work. They rush to lunch. They rush home. They hurry their dinner so they can get to their evening, then they get to bed so they can get up early and do it all over again. They are like Mike at the hospital, rushing through each given task only to be given another job he doesn't enjoy, which he can then rush to complete.

They ask, "How do you put *Clients First*?" Here they are, running a business or working for a company or practicing their chosen professions, all of which depend on clients, and they ask the question. They know they want to be treated well. They know they want to be told the truth, and they want a good job done for them, and they'd like the person taking care of them to care, but they still ask the question. They think the answer is something they can add on like a vacuum cleaner attachment or a computer module. They disconnect from the point that putting *Clients First* is the business. *Clients First* is the company; it is the only reason they have the money to make payroll. *Clients First* is the profession, for without clients to serve there is no profession. *Clients First* is a journey, not a destination.

Driven

Clients First is not a project you implement and then go on to the next fix. *Clients First* eliminates the need to fix things. My uncle used to say that a job worth doing well is worth doing twice. I was a teenager working in his service station at the time, and he was being softly sarcastic, but he gave me a sense of pride in doing a job well. *Clients First* gives you that feeling of accomplishment.

Clients First feeds upon that pride. Each time you serve a client well, it fills you up like a sugar rush, and 10 minutes later you are hungry again. You want that next client, that next opportunity. You don't have to drive yourself; *Clients First* drives you with a nagging hunger to serve.

Clients First is a journey with no end, a destination you never reach. Yet all journeys have a beginning. The steps are there. Look for that beginning to the path. Find a moment of commitment that is yours alone. Resolve to do what is right, to do whatever it takes to keep a single client. Do what is best for that person. Think only of what he or she wants, and make that goal yours. Tell the truth and serve your client. When you have done this, you make the commitment to do it again.

We build our business one client at a time. Live in the moment and serve that one client in front of you. Enjoy the journey. Forget about the clock. Manage your schedule. Be on time. But if you need to push an appointment or reschedule another client, then do it. The one thing all clients will excuse is that you are serving another client, because they know that when it is their turn you will give them the same intensity of service. You will make them number one and be 100 percent with them and their needs.

JoAnn and I have wonderful past clients. They are understanding and forgiving and patient, because they know from the previous time we served them that we treat them like the only client we have in the whole world. That is how you put *Clients First*. That is what you do.

Take that first step. Begin your journey to *Clients First*. Your life will be changed. Your present will be filled with pride, and you will find everything becoming easier. Infect all with whom you come into contact. Surround yourself with *Clients First* people. Speak your commitment and promote the three keys of *honesty*, *competence*, and *care*. You will be rewarded in every way and beyond your dreams.

Each day will be a slow trip filled with joy along the way. You will look forward to the future, but you will live in the present. You will have great memories, but they will only serve to make today better. Your clients will love you for it, and you will love them.

36 A *Clients First* World

It's 6:30 AM when the alarm goes off. Marsha rolls out of bed, giving John a shove as she heads for the bathroom. The house is quiet, because the last of the kids have moved out, but is not without excitement. John lays out Marsha's outfit, just as he's done for almost 30 years. She brings him a cup of coffee while he shaves. Their relationship is stronger than ever because they never stopped putting each other first.

At breakfast, Marsha's cell phone rings. It's Annie. She starts her first real job today at a law firm on the coast and she needs Mom's voice. "You'll be fine," Marsha says, "just remember to do your best for the clients and enjoy today. This is your *only-est* first day." She knows Annie is smiling through the phone, because "only-est" is their special word.

John works at an architectural firm downtown where he directs several projects for different clients. His team is vital to the company's success, and they are the best. They put themselves into the work and serve John because he serves them. He puts them first, and they know it. Most of his clients are past clients now, although they bring their friends with new business. John meets with these clients and then hands them off to Frank, because he knows that Frank will put their dreams first, too. When Frank won an award last year, John gave the introduction speech, in which he said that Frank was honest, competent, and caring, which was the highest praise he could think of.

Marsha has a short commute, only a mile, to her flower shop. The phone is ringing as she arrives. It's Mrs. Baker, and she is not pleased with the petunias. Although she hasn't even set down her handbag, Marsha focuses on Mrs. Baker's situation. She cares about what Mrs. Baker wants, and when Mrs. Baker asks a difficult question, Marsha trusts the truth and tells her they made a mistake. Because of Marsha's experience and because she listened, she suggests an alternative that Mrs. Baker not only likes, but likes better. Having turned lemons into lemonade, Marsha goes on with her day.

At lunch, John goes to the sporting goods store to pick up his repaired four iron. Enrico has the club back from New York, where he sourced the job to a craftsman who can perform miracles with golf equipment. The four iron, a gift from John's father, has sentimental value to him, so rather than trying to sell John a new matched set of clubs, Enrico went the extra mile to make the repair happen. Enrico knows that John knows a lot of people who play golf, and by putting John first, Enrico will have all the business he can handle.

That afternoon, Orin calls Marsha from Florida. He and Cicely and the kids are on vacation next week and plan to come for a visit. It's been a year since Marsha and John have seen their son and the grandkids. Marsha is thrilled. "Will the car make it?" she asks, and Orin says he has a new one. Yes, he went back to the same dealership as the last two times, because they treated him right, especially when the air conditioner failed on the first car. Orin works for a Fortune 500 company and has risen fast. His boss told him to take the vacation as a reward. Orin's commitment to the company, his coworkers, the folks who work on the front lines, and, ultimately, the corporation's customers was the best his boss had seen in his career. Yet Orin never got himself in his own way. With Orin, it was all about the end user and putting that person first. His boss thought that Orin might someday be CEO.

For dinner, John takes Marsha to the new bistro on Main. They celebrate the day and each other while having some wine. John is pleased to hear about Orin, and Marsha also has an update on Annie. Her first day went well, and she said when she mentioned it was all about the client in a meeting, one of the partners gave her a nod and a smile. John and Marsha count their blessings and enjoy their meal.

Fable or Fact?

Are there actually people who live this life? Are we ready for a *Clients First* world? Would we miss the drama, the egos, the dishonesty, the shoddy work, and lack of care?

Is a *Clients First* world even possible? Maybe it is and maybe it isn't. Maybe it is too much to hope that the whole world would put *Clients First*. Maybe it would be a little boring if everybody were nice, everything went well, and everyone succeeded. Perhaps we need a challenge, if only to make the victory sweeter. But, as I've told JoAnn, it's a big world.

We can sometimes feel so insignificant in the grand scheme of things. Does our vote really count? Whether we spend or don't spend that money, will it really have any effect on the economy? We are grains of sand on a very large beach.

But our world is really very small. Our world is the people we know, the place we live, where we buy our groceries, and what the weather will be where we are today. And in our world, we are not unimportant or without influence. In our world, we have the power to put *Clients First*. We have the power to put our spouses first and our kids first. We can put our neighbors first and our coworkers first. We have the power to create a *Clients First* world. We can do it one client, one customer, one boss, one employee, and one person at a time.

You have the power within you to make the commitment to *Clients First*. You can speak that commitment and influence others to put *Clients First*. You can create your own *Clients First* world. You have the power.

A *Clients First* world would be a good world—one in which everyone enjoyed the journey.

The conversation continues at:

www.ClientsFirstBook.com

- Catch the wave - Join the movement.

- See what's happening in **the Clients First World**.

- Track Joseph and JoAnn's appearance calendar.

- Check in at our blog—post reviews and/or comments.

- Tell us your Clients First miracle stories.

- Share your thoughts—get involved

- Let's create a **Clients First World**...

Thank you

for reading our Clients First story.

We would love to hear from you. E-mail us at
JoAnn@ClientsFirstBook.com
Joseph@ClientsFirstBook.com

Index